ROCKHOUNDING
Wisconsin

A Guide to the State's Best Sites

ROBERT BEARD

GUILFORD, CONNECTICUT

To the memory of my grandmother, Ruth Ware (1910–1996). She was the first rockhound that I ever knew, and she loved northern Wisconsin and geology. She would have been thrilled to read this book.

FALCONGUIDES®

An imprint of The Rowman and Littlefield Publishing Group, Inc.
4501 Forbes Blvd., Ste. 200
Lanham, MD 20706
www.rowman.com

Falcon, FalconGuides, and Make Adventure Your Story are registered trademarks of The Rowman and Littlefield Publishing Group, Inc.

Distributed by NATIONAL BOOK NETWORK

British Library Cataloguing-in-Publication Information available

Library of Congress Cataloging-in-Publication Data

Names: Beard, Robert D., author.
Title: Rockhounding Wisconsin : a guide to the state's best sites / Robert Beard.
Description: Guilford, Connecticut : FalconGuides, [2018] | Includes bibliographical references and index.
Identifiers: LCCN 2017054767 (print) | LCCN 2018004230 (ebook) | ISBN 9781493028559 (e-book) | ISBN 9781493028542 (paperback) | ISBN 9781493028559 (ebook)
Subjects: LCSH: Rocks—Collection and preservation—Wisconsin—Guidebooks. | Minerals—Collection and preservation—Wisconsin—Guidebooks.
Classification: LCC QE445.W6 (ebook) | LCC QE445.W6 B43 2018 (print) | DDC 557.75—dc23
LC record available at https://lccn.loc.gov/2017054767

∞™ The paper used in this publication meets the minimum requirements of American National Standard for Information Sciences—Permanence of Paper for Printed Library Materials, ANSI/NISO Z39.48-1992.

Printed in the United States of America

CONTENTS

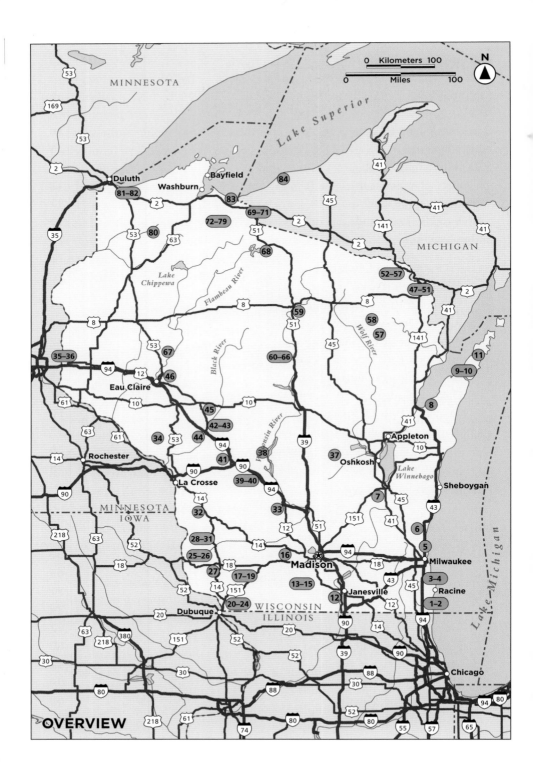

ACKNOWLEDGMENTS

Many people have helped make this book possible. I would first like to thank my editor at *Rock & Gem* magazine, Lynn Varon, who put me in contact with Globe Pequot Press, which is now Rowman & Littlefield, and William Kappele, another Rockhounding series writer and contributing editor at *Rock & Gem*, who suggested me to Lynn as a potential author for Globe Pequot in 2011. My writing experience with *Rock & Gem* has greatly expanded my capabilities as a geologist and has been a great asset to my career.

I would like to thank my editor at Rowman, David Legere, for his encouragement and support for the book, Melissa Baker in the map department, and Meredith Dias in the production department, who gave me helpful comments and suggestions. Thanks are also due to the production staff at Newgen and the many people who were instrumental in producing and distributing the book.

In the course of this work, I used many excellent online resources and websites. I benefited greatly from the work and writings of Dr. William Cordua from the University of Wisconsin-River Falls, Dr. Steven Dutch of the University of Wisconsin-Green Bay, and Dr. Thomas Fitz of Northland College in Ashland. The Institute on Lake Superior Geology had many excellent guidebooks and articles. Publications from the United States Geological Survey (USGS) and the Wisconsin Department of Natural Resources (WDNR) were extremely useful. I did my best to cite and list all of my references I used in this book, so for those whose work I referenced, thank you very much for all your work.

While in the field I did not meet many other rockhounds, but a discussion I had with the Miller family in Kenosha proved useful for my work along Lake Michigan. Jody Smale from the Pennsylvania Geological Survey library was extremely helpful with providing Wisconsin publications.

I also appreciated all the support that my friends from the Central Pennsylvania Rock and Mineral Club and the Harrisburg Area Geological Society gave when they learned that I was working on this book. I also owe thanks to Google Maps and the USGS who made the online mapping software and online geologic information that made this publication possible. Finding sites and determining the host rock geology would not be easy without these tools.

Lastly, I would like to thank my wife, Rosalina; my son, Daniel; my daughter, Roberta; and my mother, Nancy Beard. During the research for this book, they came with me on several trips. My late father, John Beard, hated coming on field trips but he always encouraged me to write and pursue my work in geology. My late grandmother, Ruth Ware, to whom this book is dedicated, also deserves many thanks for buying a lakefront cabin in northern Wisconsin in the 1960s. This has been an important place for our family and our relatives and gave me the opportunity to explore Wisconsin over many years.

I hope that you, your friends, and your families use this guide to find good field trips that become among your most memorable experiences.

INTRODUCTION

This book is for the rockhound or geologist who wants to visit sites without advance arrangements. Virtually every type of rockhounding trip can be found in this book. Some sites will allow you to park and pick up rocks as soon as you get out of your car. Other sites require some walking, and some sites require strenuous hiking over bad terrain. Some sites do not allow rock collecting at all, but are still worth visiting. At some sites you will likely find lots of minerals or fossils, and at others you may have to work hard to find anything. I have done my best to help you easily find these sites and let you know what to expect.

Wisconsin is a large state with a rich history in agriculture, manufacturing, and mining. The geology varies considerably in the state. The southern and eastern sections of the state are primarily early Paleozoic sediments, which have many locations for fossils. The southwestern corner of the state is underlain by early Paleozoic sediments and has important historic mining districts for lead and zinc. The northern and northwestern sections of the state are primarily Precambrian granitic and metamorphic rocks that are often covered by glacial sediments. The Precambrian rocks have many interesting localities for metallic and nonmetallic minerals, especially in the former iron-mining districts.

Wisconsin takes its natural resources and tourist industries seriously. The state has gone a long way in preserving land to insure public use and access. Hunting and fishing are major industries and most public lands are open to both, with some restrictions on hunting near populated places. This has helped greatly in being able to access public lands. However, in nearly all cases, mineral and fossil collecting is either discouraged or entirely prohibited on state and other public lands in Wisconsin.

I have focused on identifying sites that you can visit by yourself or with your family without significant advance planning or permission. I have personally checked every one of the sites in this book. I also visited many sites that were notable for their absence of minerals or fossils and have excluded those from the book. Many of the sites are roadcuts or outcrops that are limited in size but still worth visiting.

Roadcuts are often within the highway right-of-way and sometimes belong to the state or local government. Generally you can collect in these areas if they are safe, not disrupting traffic, and clearly not marked against entry. I have never had a problem with collecting at roadcuts, but always make certain that I am not inside posted ground and that I am not in an area where I am posing a risk to traffic. Collecting on interstate highways is illegal, so I do not have any sites along interstate highways in this book.

Land and access status can change at any time. Even if a private site is not posted, this guide does not imply or suggest that collecting at the site is permitted. Many entries in this book are in city parks, county parks, state forests, state parks, federal lands, or other places that are accessible to the public, and while you can go to these sites, rock collecting is prohibited in many of them. Collecting rules are not applied uniformly in many cases. If you look at the park regulations, you may find that any ground disturbance, including picking up a rock, is prohibited.

Many of these same parks and state agencies publish field guides to these parks. In these cases you will have to use your best judgment as to whether or not to collect rocks if you visit a site. If there are signs clearly stating "no mineral collecting," do not collect rocks. Likewise, if you are in a place where you know collecting is forbidden, you can look at the rocks, but do not collect them. Wisconsin state parks, while offering excellent access to see former mines, quarries, and outcrops, do not allow any collecting. Where an interesting mineral or fossil occurrence is on publicly accessible land but collecting is prohibited, I have still listed it in this book if I have visited it and consider the locality worth a visit. I have not yet found a site where it is against the law to look at the rocks, but I am increasingly finding sites where even photography requires a permit.

I have stayed away from listing mine and quarry sites where you have to obtain advance permission and appointments, as readers may not be able to schedule and make advance arrangements. Quarries and mines are generally best visited as a group with a local mineral club or other organizations. Such group trips to quarries could be well worth your time, as you'll bypass identifying landowners and permission issues. However, you must be sure to bring your own hard hat, steel-toed boots, hammer, and other tools needed for the rocks you encounter. Active quarries in Wisconsin are great collecting sites when you can get in, but many of the quarries do not allow mineral collecting.

For the rockhound with family members who don't love rocks quite as much as you do, this book also includes local attractions near each site.

Many of these are local state parks, natural areas, nearby lakes, and nearby city attractions. These should help you plan a trip that's fun for everyone. At a minimum you can at least say that you made an effort to find some other activities besides looking at rocks.

Wisconsin is a big state, and it is nearly impossible to cover every locality. While I attempted to include as many sites as possible in this book, I found that the list of good sites kept growing, and eventually I had to draw the line on adding localities. The good news is that the more I kept looking, the more sites I kept finding. This is important, as it shows that there are still more sites to visit. I have never run out of new places to find rocks.

The best way to start this hobby is to go out and look for rocks. You and your companions will see some interesting geology and places and have some shared experiences, which hopefully will be positive.

ROCKHOUNDING BASICS

Rockhounding can be a low-budget hobby. The entry requirements are minimal. All you need are your eyes and hands to see and pick up interesting rocks. However, as you advance you'll want some additional tools.

COLLECTING EQUIPMENT

A good **hammer** is the most important tool for the rockhound. I recommend a rock-pick hammer with a pointed tip. Hardware stores don't usually carry these, but they are available at some surveying supply shops, at rock shows, and online. My preferred brand is an Estwing foot-long hammer with a pointed tip and a Shock Reduction Grip. I have used mine for over thirty years. It is almost impossible to destroy, despite thousands of whacks against very hard rocks and lots of time outside in the rain and snow. Do not use a regular claw hammer. The steel splinters that break off the hammer head when you hit a hard rock are dangerous. Unlike sparks, which can also occur, you cannot see the splinters. You should also be aware that similar splinters will often shoot off a new rock hammer when you are first using it against hard rocks.

If you are hammering, it is also critical to wear **safety glasses or goggles**. I wear glasses normally to see, and my glasses have often been damaged by flying rock chips and steel hammer splinters. In the event that I am hammering large rocks on a constant basis, such as in a quarry, I will cover my glasses with safety goggles. When collecting in urban environments, rocks are often associated with broken glass, which becomes another hazard when hit with a hammer.

I also use a **chisel** to help break apart rocks when needed, but many chisels have very wide blades and are difficult to use when splitting the soft, finely bedded sediments that are common in many fossiliferous shales. I sometimes use a cheap **flat-bladed screwdriver** for soft shaly rocks where a chisel is too big to use. I know this is not the proper use of a screwdriver, but I have not found a better tool for splitting apart soft shaly rocks. Of course, if you try to use a flat-bladed screwdriver to split apart hard rocks, you really are then abusing the tool and run the risk of breaking the screwdriver or injuring yourself. When splitting harder rocks, the better tool is a chisel, and you need a narrow blade if the rocks are to be split along tight fractures.

Gloves are the next critical item. I used to do fieldwork without gloves but this was a dangerous practice. Make sure you protect your hands. All of us with jobs that involve a computer are in big trouble if we lose the use of a finger or hand. Get a good pair of heavy leather work gloves from your local hardware store. Gloves are also great when moving through briars, climbing on sharp rocks, and avoiding broken glass. It is easy to pinch your bare fingers when moving around large rocks, but gloves will help prevent this. It is better to get the end of your glove caught under a rock than the end of your finger.

Get a good pair of steel-toed or equivalent **boots** to protect your feet. Having steel-toed boots is a requirement for collecting in quarries and mines, and it is easy to find and purchase a good pair. I prefer to have relatively light-weight boots. Make sure you walk in them before purchasing.

A **hard hat**, while not needed for collecting at most roadcuts or places without overhead hazards, is equipment you should always have available. While you may not need one for casual rock collecting, you should have one with you or in your car in case you get invited to collect in a quarry or visit an active mine.

A **smartphone** is now practically a necessity. Just a couple years ago I did not have a smartphone, but now I use one all the time. It has become critical as I use Google Maps to find sites and give me real-time data on my location. I cannot believe that I used to go to the field without a smartphone. Now I cannot imagine trying to find a site without the use of satellite photographs and the Global Positioning System (GPS) in the phone.

A **field book** and a **camera** are useful for recording key site information. I like to record coordinates of sites and take notes of what I have found for future reference. I also use a small pocket-sized digital camera and often take hundreds of shots a day to increase my chances of getting that perfect shot. I use my smartphone as a backup camera, as I still prefer the pictures with my dedicated digital camera. However, I am sure that in a short time my digital camera will be replaced with my phone camera.

A **hand lens** to inspect mineral and fossils up close is also very useful, but if you are as nearsighted as I am, you can just take off your glasses and look closely. I recommend a quality hand lens that is at least 10× magnification if your natural vision is not sufficient.

Carrying your rocks from the site is often a chore. I like to use a small **backpack** when I have to walk a long distance, but sometimes a **five-gallon bucket** works best. A bucket is useful when you are picking up muddy rocks, and it is easy to put in your car. Just be careful not to break the bottom if you intend to also use it as a bucket. It is really irritating to fill your bucket with water and have it leak all over the place.

A **wagon** is good to have if you are working in quarries or places where you can expect to take out significant amounts of rocks. Collecting lots of rocks in a quarry is fine, as what you do not collect is just going to go to a crusher. If you take your wagon to a roadcut, you are collecting too many rocks. This can also attract attention from police and nosy people. Always try to keep a low profile and do not attract any unwanted attention.

GPS UNITS AND MAPS

Before digital mapping, I used to find every site by using topographic and highway maps. Now I use a handheld **GPS unit** to record key site location information, and I use the coordinate feature on my car GPS to take me to the site. I still meet people who are not using all available features of their GPS unit, such as the latitude and longitude feature, so be sure you brush up on all the available features of your GPS. Now I also use my smartphone GPS and the satellite imagery, combined with real-time tracking, is critical for finding sites. I cannot imagine rockhounding without my smartphone.

Despite the advantages of GPS units and smartphones, you should always have **maps** as a backup. I like to have a state map, and I often get free maps at rest areas. I have also found my standard US road atlas works very well. Batteries can die, and satellite and mobile signals can be dropped in wilderness and urban areas where you do not have good clearance for satellite signals. Sometimes your charger will also short out. This happened to me on a multiday collecting trip, and I felt like I was traveling blind when my GPS ran out of battery power. A good highway map can complement your GPS and help make certain that you are not taking an incorrect road. Too many people have relied solely on their GPS unit and have taken roads that were not meant for travel, especially in winter months. Unfortunately, many of these travelers died. If you get lost, most of the rockhounding trips in this book will not have such severe consequences, but never underestimate the value of a good map and never rely solely on your GPS. If possible, you should also get **topographic maps** of your site. I used to buy hard copy maps, but they are expensive, especially when you are looking at several sites. I recently bought a set of topographic maps on CD from National Geographic, but unfortunately they have discontinued the CD series and replaced them with online maps.

I found these to be completely unsuitable for my purposes, as I am often in areas without Internet access. I am hoping that technology and Internet access will improve to the point where I will access online topographic maps, but for now I am still working with my older copies on CD.

HEALTH AND SAFETY

Rockhounding presents many hazards that you will not encounter in other hobbies. In addition to having the proper gear, there are many health and safety considerations. Any time you go into the field, you are going into an uncontrolled and potentially hostile environment, and you need to take some basic steps to protect yourself and your collecting companions.

Sunscreen is one of the most effective and easy-to-use safety products, but many collectors still ignore its benefits. However, you need to put it on right away after you get to the site, or even better, before you leave the house. Many sites, especially the floors of open pit mines, act like giant solar reflectors, and the sun can be very intense. I also highly recommend a good pair of dark **sunglasses**. I cannot spend any time at all in an area of light-colored rocks if I do not have my sunglasses. Likewise, if you are not wearing a hard hat, wear a baseball cap or other hat for protection from the sun.

Although the sun is often an issue, rain is often a bigger issue. I highly recommend having an **umbrella** handy. I know it sounds ridiculous, but I have gone on many extended hikes in the woods in driving rain with an umbrella, and this helped a great deal. An umbrella can make a big difference in the quality of your trip, especially when you are with friends or kids who may not enjoy a soaking rainstorm.

Speaking of rain, **lightning** can be a significant concern. Many of the sites in this book are often exposed to strong thunderstorms and lightning. An umbrella will not help you if there is lightning. The best defense is to monitor the local forecast and get to a safe place long before the lightning arrives. Assuming you have a smartphone, you should be able to view radar maps that can warn you in advance of approaching storms. Your car will protect you from lightning, but bear in mind that most thunderstorms also come with strong winds, and you have to stay away from trees that can blow down on your vehicle. Every year people in the region are killed by both lightning strikes and falling trees.

Poison ivy can be a serious problem in Wisconsin. Poison ivy usually grows on the borders of outcrops and rocks, and this is another good reason to wear gloves. In fact, if your gloves have had extensive contact with the poison ivy, you may just have to throw them away.

While I always enjoy collecting in shorts and short-sleeve shirts, many sites are hidden among briars and other plants that can make your experience miserable if your legs and arms are exposed. I recommend always having a pair of **long pants** and a **light jacket** available if you need it, and you can also anticipate that these clothes will soon get ripped to shreds by thorns, broken branches, and sharp rocks. Long pants and sleeves can also help protect you from the sun and insects as well as flying rock chips and steel splinters from hammering.

Ticks are a major concern. During tick season, which seems to vary from place to place, I often find that I have been exposed to ticks as I am driving away from the site and see several crawling on my arms and legs just as I am entering traffic. Lyme disease is a serious issue, and you have to be on your guard at all times. The larger wood ticks, while not aesthetically pleasing, are typically not carriers of Lyme disease, while the much smaller deer ticks are known carriers. Rocky Mountain spotted fever, another serious tick-borne illness, is often carried by dog ticks, which are much larger than deer ticks. If you find a tick embedded in you, you may be at risk. Some say that it has to be there for 24 hours, but studies have shown that Lyme can be transmitted much sooner. Keep an eye on the bite mark, and contact your physician if it gets worse over the next few days.

To remove a tick, grasp the skin around the insertion of the tick with a pair of fine-point tweezers and pull straight outward, but be careful not to squeeze the tick body, as it may inject germs into the skin. Do not traumatize the tick with a lit match or cigarette. A traumatized tick can regurgitate its bacteria-laden stomach contents back into you. You will then be at greater risk of a tick-transmitted disease.

Using an insect repellant that contains **N,N-Diethyl-*meta*-toluamide**, which is better known as DEET or **diethyltoluamide**, is a good defense, as is light-colored clothing so you can quickly spot and remove the ticks. But even with insect repellent, you can still get bitten. I received a Lyme tick bite in 2013 and had a bright red circle on my shoulder almost immediately, despite being covered with insect repellent. My doctor put me on antibiotics and apparently this took care of it, but I never even saw the tick.

Insect repellant with DEET is also good to keep away the **mosquitoes**, which may be present at any sites near standing water. Mosquitoes can also come out in force a few days after heavy rains. I have been on many trips that were nearly ruined because I did not have ready access to insect repellant. Insect repellant wipes are also good to keep in your backpack if you are prone to forgetting repellant or if you do not want to carry around an entire bottle of repellant. West Nile virus, which is carried by mosquitoes, is a serious threat. Spraying by state authorities has often dramatically reduced the numbers of mosquitoes, but if you are in an area that has not been sprayed and the mosquitoes are out, you will be in for a miserable trip if you are not protected. In extreme cases a mosquito net might be appropriate, but I have not been in any parts of Wisconsin where I felt a net was necessary, and insect repellant has always seemed to be sufficient.

Wildlife is also an issue in Wisconsin. Recently we visited a site with lots of **snakes**, but fortunately we were not bitten. While collecting in some of the remote areas of northern Wisconsin you may also come across **bears**. We also saw a **wolf** one evening crossing a road, but the biggest hazard when driving are **deer**, especially at night. Put your cell phone away and always focus on the road.

An **orange or yellow safety vest** is important for any site where you are collecting along a roadside or any site that may be exposed to traffic or heavy equipment. Roads will always be dangerous, and many of the sites in this guide are at roadcuts. Provided you park in a safe place and stay well off the road, you should not have a problem, and the safety vest may alert traffic to your presence. You should always make sure cars see you, especially if your back is turned and you cannot see them. An orange vest may be a state requirement if you are anywhere near a wooded area during hunting season. Generally I stay out of the woods during any gun hunting season. Curious onlookers may also assume that you are a highway worker or other employee just out doing their job and not question why you are so intently studying a roadcut.

Dehydration and **hunger** can make you and your companions miserable. Make sure that you and your collecting companions bring enough bottled water, and if you will be out all day, bring something to eat. Nearly all of the sites described in this guidebook are close to cities and places where you can get lunch, and most trips are half-day trips, so hunger is generally not a problem. Water, however, can be a problem. I generally have at least one ½ liter of bottled water in my backpack and often take two ½ liters of bottled water, and make sure that my collecting companions also have bottled water. I know this sounds obvious, but it is not a good situation to be miles from the car and not have water for a thirsty person that you have introduced to rockhounding. Never, ever drink water from streams, no matter how remote or how good it looks, unless you are equipped with a proper filter.

Getting to the site safely is important. The parking areas for the sites in this book can all be easily reached with a two-wheel-drive vehicle. It seems obvious, but if you are driving to a site, be sure your vehicle will get you there and that you have **plenty of gas**. I always try to keep my tank topped off. Gas stations are relatively easy to find, but I do not like it when my tank gets low. If you are taking more than one vehicle, make certain that there will be enough parking for two cars. Many drives are also very long, so if you get tired, be sure to pull over at a secure rest area and take a break.

While many collecting sites are in somewhat rural areas, some of the sites in this book are in urban settings. You should always be aware of your surroundings, make sure your vehicle is parked in a secure place, keep your vehicle GPS hidden, do not leave valuables visible in your car, and be alert for suspicious characters. Generally, if you have a bad feeling about where you parked your car, you will find that feeling has been justified when you return.

Underground mines are generally a nonissue in Wisconsin, as most of the unstable mines collapsed or were closed many decades ago, and many of the open mines now have bat gates or other structures that keep people out. However, it is still possible to come across open portals and shafts. Many of the former quarries also have high walls over 50 feet high. The best policy is to stay outside of any underground workings and to be extra careful when you are collecting at a quarry.

Finally, you have to be careful when dealing with sites on **private property**. Always ask permission when you can, and be prepared to get yelled at or have other unpleasant experiences with landowners. Many of my most unpleasant experiences have involved dealing with large vicious dogs. Nearly all the landowners I have talked with have been good about giving permission, but every now and then I come across unfriendly owners. This challenge comes with the hobby, so if you are going to look for rocks on private lands and ask their owners for access, you have to be ready to deal with difficult people.

IMPORTANT ONLINE TOOLS

Many mineral and fossil localities have recently disappeared into developments, yet in that same time frame it's become much easier to find new sites. Google,

Yahoo, Bing, Google Earth, Google Maps, and other such online resources can be accessed to identify sites and explore potential localities.

I have found Google Maps to be especially helpful and always check the site using both the map and the satellite views. The map views are great, as they usually indicate the street names and boundaries of public property, such as local and state parks. The satellite views are extremely useful, as you can zoom in and clearly see key items such as open pits, mine dumps, and signs of disturbance that may indicate historic or recent soil excavation and movement. Many sites, especially when minerals or fossils cover a broad area, are often exposed unexpectedly, and the satellite views in Google Maps can be a quick check to see recent exposures. Unfortunately these are not real-time photographs, and they are generally at least a year or two old. However, they are still much better than many maps and aerial photographs that may be decades old.

I have purposely left most website addresses and phone numbers out of this guide, as web addresses expire, phone numbers change, and it is usually easy to find a web address via a search engine. Running an Internet search on a locality often brings up new and important updates, especially if a site has changed land status.

Likewise, all of the references cited in this book refer to the actual publication and do not provide a web address for access, unless the only available reference is the website itself. If you type in the citations or key parts of them, you can often access them online. If not, you can generally get them through your state library. I have found that a few publications are now only available on microfiche, but your librarian can often arrange for a copy to be e-mailed to you.

GEOLOGY OF WISCONSIN

Some basic understanding of Wisconsin geology will help you understand why you encounter certain rocks, minerals, and fossils in various parts of the state. Wisconsin has five main geographic provinces. These are the Eastern Ridges and Lowlands, the Western Upland, the Central Plain, Northern Highland, and Lake Superior Lowland, and a description of each follows.

EASTERN RIDGES AND LOWLANDS

The Eastern Ridges and Lowlands province is mainly a flat, eastward sloping plain with two ridges that trend in broad arc from southern Wisconsin to northeast Wisconsin. The eastern ridge is Silurian dolostone. This ridge is known as the Niagara escarpment and it is sometimes referred to as the backbone of the Door County peninsula. This rock unit actually extends in a much broader area through Michigan and into New York. The western ridge is Ordovician limestone, and is known as the Black River Escarpment. Much of the lowlands between and east of the ridges were carved out by glaciers, especially in the northern part of the province.

The bedrock of this province is primarily Silurian and Ordovician carbonates. The area is well suited for agriculture, and most of the largest cities in Wisconsin, including Milwaukee, Kenosha, Racine, Madison, Sheboygan, Appleton, and Green Bay are in this province. The area has some interesting fossil collecting localities near Lake Michigan and some former iron mines. Roadcuts tend to be scarce due to the low relief and glacial deposits that cover much of the bedrock.

WESTERN UPLAND

The Western Upland covers much of western Wisconsin. Like many upland areas, rivers and streams have cut deeply into the terrain. The area has many cliffs and rock outcroppings, which make it an interesting area for rockhounding.

Much of the Western Upland is part of the Driftless Area, which is a region that was not covered by glaciers during the ice age. The Driftless Area does not have the broad glacial carved valleys or the extensive cover of glacial sediments that are found in previously glaciated parts of Wisconsin. The valleys in the Driftless Area of the Western Upland were formed by streams and

Snakes are common in many areas of Wisconsin and it is best to leave them undisturbed.

rivers, not glaciers. Huge cliffs are present along the Mississippi and Wisconsin Rivers, as well many smaller waterways and highways.

Most of the Western Upland is underlain by Ordovician and Cambrian sediments. Many of these are fossiliferous limestones and dolostones with abundant chert. Sandstone is abundant and many of the sandstone cliffs are bright white to orange, and often have excellent cross-bedding.

The Western Upland also hosts the Upper Mississippi Valley lead–zinc mining district in southwestern Wisconsin. From the early nineteenth to mid-twentieth century, this was one of the most important lead–zinc districts of the United States. Nearly all of the mines are on private land or have been completely reclaimed, but roadcuts and waste rock piles still provide inter-esting collecting opportunities.

THE CENTRAL PLAIN

The Central Plain is a broad, crescent–shaped section that is mostly underlain by Cambrian sandstone, except in the western end where Precambrian basaltic rocks are exposed. The sandstone is not resistant to erosion when compared to

Porcupines are a common site in many areas of Wisconsin and you must be careful to keep dogs and children from getting too curious.

many other rocks. Erosion has left elevated sections of the sandstone, known locally as mounds, above the plains. This has resulted in a landscape of flat monotonous plains dotted with mounds of sandstone. Some of the sandstone mounds also have prominent cliffs.

The flat plains of the Central Plain were formed largely by glacial meltwaters that washed sandy sediments out from the base of the glaciers. Some of these formed lakes, which enabled the sediments to settle and form broad, flat expanses. One of the biggest was formed about 20,000 years ago when the main basin of Glacial Lake Wisconsin filled with glacial meltwater. This lake was nearly the size of the current Great Salt Lake in Utah, and the lake effectively kept the glaciers out the driftless areas of the Central Plains and the Western Upland. About 18,000 years ago the ice dam broke, and the lake quickly drained. The flooding must have been devastating to everything below the ice dam. The resulting flow helped define much of the landscape of the Wisconsin River and other rivers and streams of the region. Mineral collecting is limited to the Cambrian sandstones and some of the Precambrian rocks exposed beneath the sandstones.

These deer were next to an iron mine dump in the Northern Highland. Deer pose a threat when driving almost anywhere in Wisconsin.

NORTHERN HIGHLAND

The Northern Highland covers much of northern Wisconsin, and it is known for its forests and swamps. The region has the oldest rocks in Wisconsin and nearly all of the bedrock is Precambrian igneous and metamorphic rock and minor exposures of Cambrian sediments. The Northern Highland is within the southern end of the Canadian Shield. The Canadian Shield is a vast extent of Precambrian rocks that forms the core of northern North America.

The Northern Highland, like many regions of Precambrian rocks, was previously mountainous. It was submerged by early Paleozoic seas as the mountains were eroded. About 200 million years ago the area was uplifted and remained above the early seas while much of what became southern Wisconsin was submerged. Erosion was slow to cut into the hard granite and gneisses, but it had millions and millions of years to do so. Much of the Northern Highland was covered by glaciers, which left extensive glacial drift deposits and carved the hundreds of lakes in the Highlands.

The highest point in Wisconsin, Timms Hill in Price County, is 1,952 feet above mean sea level. Timms Hill consists of a thick accumulation of glacial debris. Try to imagine how high the glaciers much have been, if the glacial debris now forms the highest point in the state. It is also important to note that a small section of the Northern Highland in Marathon County is also in the Driftless Area, and this shows what some of the area was like without the effects of glaciation.

Rock collecting in the Northern Highland is often excellent, when you can find rocks. The area is thickly covered by forests, glacial drift, lakes, and swamps, and outcrops are hard to find. When you find an outcrop you need to make the most of it.

The primary metallic minerals for collectors in the region are iron minerals, which are mainly hematite and magnetite. Some copper mineralization occurs in the region but many of the copper mines are long gone or reclaimed. There are also many good occurrences of coarse feldspars, pyroxenes, garnet, and kyanite. Some tourmaline is also found in pegmatites and metamorphic rocks. The Northern Highland is a major tourist destination and has many hiking trails, waterfalls, boat landings, and even swimming beaches in some of the sandier lakes.

LAKE SUPERIOR LOWLAND

The Lake Superior Lowland is the smallest of the geographic provinces, and is located in the northern end of Wisconsin along Lake Superior. It is sometimes referred to as the Superior Coastal Plain. It is best defined as a plain that slopes from the Northern Highland to Lake Superior. The bedrock is nearly all Middle Proterozoic Chequamegon Sandstone of the Bayfield Group, which is primarily arkose. The Lowland is generally covered by woods down to Lake Superior, and the coastline generally is defined by cliffs of soft arkose.

For mineral collectors, the Lake Superior Lowland is best known as a key location for Lake Superior agates. The best agates come from weathered basalts, so it is important to understand the regional geology and focus on areas near the sources of the agates. According to geologic maps of the region by the USGS, most of the basaltic rocks that could be potential source rocks are located near the Michigan border with Wisconsin and near the Amnicon River in Douglas County.

NATURAL RESOURCES

Wisconsin was a significant producer of metallic and nonmetallic minerals. The state is nicknamed "The Badger State" after the nineteenth-century miners in southwestern Wisconsin that dug holes like badgers in search of lead ore. Today mining is largely limited to construction aggregates, specialty industrial minerals, and sand for hydraulic fracturing in the oil and gas industry. When collecting minerals and fossils, it is important to understand the underlying reasons for the location of mines and quarries. This will often help you identify the types of rocks you will encounter and give you some history lessons at the same time.

LEAD

Lead was the first metal mined in significant quantities in Wisconsin. The lead deposits are part of the Upper Mississippi lead-zinc district. The deposits are mainly in Ordovician carbonates and occur as gash-filled veins, replacement masses, and along bedding planes and fractures. Galena was the main lead mineral that was mined, and the gangue minerals included calcite, marcasite, and pyrite.

Lead ores were discovered in the late 1820s in southwestern Wisconsin, and the mines were developed rapidly. The lead ores were near the surface and were smelted to produce lead that was processed into pewter, pipes, weights, paint, and bullets. By 1829 more than 4,000 miners worked the deposits, and produced nearly 13 million pounds of lead annually. Town and community names like Mineral Point, New Diggings, Lead Mine, and Potosi are all reminders of a the region's mining history.

Lead mining peaked by about 1844. The easily found lead ores near the surface had been mined out. Miners soon left for copper and iron mines that were being developed elsewhere in Wisconsin and in other states. The real kicker was when gold was discovered in California in 1849. Miners who had been barely making a living out scraping lead from the ground undoubtedly thought they could strike it rich in California, especially with their mining expertise. While mining experience certainly helped, most of them likely suffered the same destitution and poverty of the majority of the 49ers.

Although lead is extremely toxic, many of the former lead districts later became some of America's most productive agriculture lands. Dairy and cheese became and still remain major industries in southwestern Wisconsin. The mining of lead largely ended before technology could aid in extracting and processing more lead. This may have been fortuitous, for if lead mining had gone on to the present day, southwest Wisconsin might be known more for toxic lead waste than cheese.

Nearly all of the lead mines are long closed, and the remaining surface workings are almost entirely reclaimed or capped with soil cover. Unless you obtain permission to access one of the very few remaining mine sites, it is difficult to collect at former mines. The best odds for finding lead ores in southwest Wisconsin are to look in roadcuts and piles of waste rocks that may be on highway or public right of ways. Roadcuts, unfortunately, are few and far between as much of the region is fairly flat.

ZINC

Miners were certainly attracted to the silvery galena found in the near surface lead ores, and they also mined the unusual zinc carbonate smithsonite that was associated with the surface ores. As they mined deeper, they had to be intrigued by the heavy, soft brown mineral with a yellow brown streak and sulfur smell they encountered below the galena. This was quickly identified as sphalerite, which is a principal ore of zinc.

After the Civil War the economy began to recover, and many of the former lead mines were soon operated for zinc. Zinc was an important component of brass, which is a metal alloy of copper and zinc, and it is a strong and decorative metal used for many purposes. Zinc oxide could also be used in paint. With westward expansion and the greater demand for metal parts and construction, the focus in the southwestern Wisconsin mines shifted to zinc. Sphalerite was not as easy to process as the oxidized ores of smithsonite, but the economics soon made it possible to expand many of the mines and bring in new processes. Zinc mining continued until about the 1920s.

Just like the lead mines, most of the former zinc mines are also on private lands and have been long closed or reclaimed. Your best opportunities for finding sphalerite and related minerals are to look in roadcuts and waste rock piles.

IRON

Iron has a long and important history as a metal mined in Wisconsin, but development of the iron deposits did not occur until the mid-1800s. Deposits were first worked in southern Wisconsin and later in northeastern and north-western Wisconsin. The iron was initially produced in furnaces near the mines. Wisconsin had lots of limestone but very little coal. The iron ores were also different from those of early mines of the eastern United States, which were the main sources of the iron production in the late 1700s to early 1800s. The ores in the eastern United States were often bog iron and near surface masses of goethite and limonite ores, which were abundant and easily worked. In contrast, the first Wisconsin ores that were processed were either sedimentary hematitic ores or hematite-magnetite sedimentary iron formation.

Iron ore was reportedly first discovered in 1839 in the Black River Falls area. These deposits were Precambrian iron formation. The deposits were worked by 1849, and plans for much a larger mining operation were developed by 1860. The investors sent a buyer and their money to Milwaukee to buy machinery for the mine. Unfortunately the buyer went for a short cruise on the steamer *Lady Elgin*. This turned out to be the final voyage for the *Lady Elgin*, as the steamer was rammed by another ship and sank in a major gale. The buyer and the money for the machinery went to the bottom of Lake Michigan. This bankrupted the operation, and iron mining at Black River Falls was halted for decades.

In the meantime other iron ore deposits were developed in Dodge County to the east. The Mayville and Iron Ridge mines in Dodge County were developed in the mid-nineteenth century, and iron was mined at Mayville until 1928 and at Iron Ridge until 1914. These were mainly hematitic ores that developed in the Silurian dolostone of the Niagara Escarpment, which is a prominent ridge that extends from southern Wisconsin to the Door County peninsula and beyond.

In Sauk County, the Baraboo iron-mining district was developed in the early 1900s. These deposits were mainly siderite and hematite that formed in Precambrian slate, chert, and dolostone. These deposits were worked near the surface and the workings generally did not extend more than 500 feet. The ores were soon worked out and the mines closed by the mid-1920s.

The Menominee Range iron deposits in northeastern Wisconsin were known before the Civil War, but mining was not started until the 1870s. The mines were in the Menominee River valley, and a limited number of mines were developed south of the Michigan border near Florence. The mines had to compete with larger deposits in Michigan, and mine economics soon resulted in the Wisconsin mines closing.

The Gogebic Range deposits in northwestern Wisconsin were discovered around 1882 and were soon developed into major iron mines. The ore belt extended into the Upper Peninsula of Michigan as well. The Gogebic Range was one of America's main sources of iron from the late 1800s into the 1920s. The deposits found it difficult to complete with other larger deposits in Minnesota and Michigan, and with the Great Depression many of the mines closed forever.

From 2010 to 2015 there was considerable interest in developing a new large open pit iron mine in the Gogebic Range. This would have been a huge deep open pit mine, and it would have taken out much of the iron ore in the iron formation that makes up the Gogebic Range in northwestern Wisconsin. The mine was controversial due to its extreme size and potential environmental consequences. On the positive side, it would have put these iron reserves to industrial use and created an economic boom for northwestern Wisconsin. On the negative side, the area would have changed forever, and many of its environmental consequences cannot be foreseen. The company developing the mine withdrew its application for the mine in 2015, so for now the area remains undeveloped with any new iron mines.

COPPER

Copper was likely the first metal mined in Wisconsin. Native Americans picked up native copper on the shores of Lake Superior in prehistoric times. Copper jewelry dating from 4,000 to 1,200 BC from Wisconsin and Michigan came from these deposits. This is often referred to as the "Old Copper Culture." The early French traders saw the large pieces of native copper and recognized their significance, and early attempts at systematic mining began in the mid-eighteenth century. However, the easy copper was undoubtedly soon depleted. The area was a hard place to make a living, and settlers scraped by on the fur trade, timber, and supporting the early ports of Lake Superior.

By the mid-1800s there was a renewed interest in mining the iron ores discovered in northern Wisconsin. This was due to the depletion of the lead ores in southwest Wisconsin, the rise in interest in mining due to the discovery of the gold fields in California, and perhaps most importantly, the Federal Government's push to kick the remaining Indians in Wisconsin out to lands west of the Mississippi. Attempts were made to develop the copper deposits in the basalts of northwestern Wisconsin, but none of these developed into major mines. Iron was still king and would dominate northern

Wisconsin mining until the early twentieth century. Attempt to mine small occurrences of copper in southwestern Wisconsin also did not result in any major mines.

In the mid–1900s advances in geophysics and remote sensing led to important copper discoveries in northern Wisconsin. Many of these were massive sulfide bodies with millions of tons of relatively high grade of copper ore, and these were buried under glacial debris and swamps. They were later confirmed by drilling. In addition to copper, many of these deposits had significant amounts of gold and silver.

The Flambeau Mine deposit, located in Flambeau, was confirmed in 1968 by core drilling. Indications that the deposit existed were based on anomalies detected in an Aero-Electromagnetic (AEM) survey of the area. The mine was not permitted and developed until 1993. It operated until 1997 and produced 181,000 tons of copper, 334,000 ounces of gold, and 3.3 million ounces of silver. It was reclaimed immediately afterward. The owner, Rio Tinto, uses it an example of proper mine reclamation, while opponents claim that the mining has resulted in groundwater contamination.

Other proposed copper mines, most notably the Crandon deposit, were not able to obtain permits for mining and the owners subsequently cancelled the projects. For now, metallic mineral mining in Wisconsin is still on hold, but attempts continue to be made to obtain approval for several mines. For the copper mineral collector, these mines will not be open for a long time, if they are ever developed, and access will likely be problematic even if the mines open.

CONSTRUCTION AGGREGATES

Wisconsin has a strong construction aggregates industry. The bedrock and surficial geology are ideal for quarries and pits for crushed stone, sand and gravel, rip-rap, and dimension stone. Quarries are all over Wisconsin, and the bedrock determines the type of quarry and the rock that is produced. Quarries that are in Paleozoic carbonates generally produce crushed stone, and pits that are in glacial deposits produce sand and gravel. These materials go into ready-mix concrete, asphalt, and roads. In some cases quarries that produce very large hard dense rocks do not crush them but use them for stream and lake stabilization as rip-rap. The shores of Lake Michigan and Lake Superior are lined in many areas with millions of tons of boulders to protect against the strong waves of the Great Lakes.

Transportation is a limiting factor and most construction aggregate remains in local markets. It is important to note that there are no active cement manufacturing plants in Wisconsin. The cement industry used to be significant, especially in the Milwaukee area, but the deposits were mined out or otherwise became uneconomic. The lack of in-state cement resources has led to occasional cement shortages for the construction industry.

HYDRAULIC FRACTURING SAND

Wisconsin has outstanding deposits of Cambrian and early Paleozoic sandstones that are ideal for hydraulic fracturing sand. Hydraulic fracturing sand is used in the oil and gas industry as a proppant to hold open geologic formations when they are fractured by injecting water and sand under high pressure thousands of feet underground. Nearly all of the sand mining operations are located in western and southwestern Wisconsin. Hydraulic fracturing sand is difficult to make from materials other than the pure, well-rounded and well-sized sand that nature made hundreds of millions of years ago. Unfortunately, while this has resulted in opening new mines and providing new jobs, there is considerable opposition to these new mines. The biggest complaints involve the silica dust and the fact that the sand is being mined to support the fossil fuel industry.

ROOFING GRANULES

Roofing granules are another important material mined and processed in Wisconsin. One of the largest granule producers is located in northeastern Wisconsin and mines and processes a Precambrian meta-andesite. Other granule producers process slag and other materials for granules and abrasives. Roofing granules and abrasives are important industries in Wisconsin and these tend to be among the more stable businesses in the mining industry.

HOW TO USE THIS GUIDE

The sites are listed by their location in the physiographic provinces, and generally are numbered westward from east to west and are grouped by geologic province. Site names are often based on the nearest town, but in some cases I have used a local geographic feature for the locality name, especially if this will help collectors with locating the site. Maps with the localities have also been provided to help you plan site visits.

Each site entry gives **GPS coordinates** for parking, and if necessary, coordinates for the site itself, should you need to hike there. The coordinates are the latitude and longitude and are provided in the degrees–decimal minutes format in the World Geodetic System (WGS 84) datum. The coordinates are rounded to three decimal points. Enter the coordinates in your GPS device, and it will take your vehicle to the site. You must make certain that you are entering the coordinates in the correct format, and your GPS unit should be easy to convert to degrees–decimal minutes. However, be aware that some GPS systems will take you on back roads and trails, and these may not be the best route to the site. In some cases, especially in rural and mountainous areas, they may take you on roads and trails that are not maintained or not made for motor vehicles.

Make sure that you understand how to use your GPS, especially when using coordinates. For some reason, some users know how to enter a street address but do not know how to enter a latitude and longitude. While this guidebook gives latitude and longitude in degrees–decimal minutes, other guides may give coordinates in degrees decimal or degrees-minutes-seconds, and you have to understand what you are entering into your GPS unit. While your unit may be able to do the conversion, you may have to do a conversion to the correct format yourself, but this is simple, provided you understand basic algebra. Often the GPS will give you a preview of where you are going after you enter the coordinates, and you should check this to see if it looks correct. If it is taking you out to Lake Michigan, into a big field, or into a bunch of buildings in Milwaukee, you may have entered the coordinates incorrectly. It is easy to make this type of mistake, but fortunately this is easy to fix, provided you catch it before you go too far.

The **finding the site** section can be a good partner to your GPS as you plan your trip. In this section, a route to each site is given from a major highway or, occasionally, from a nearby city. Depending on where you have started, the site may be between you and that starting point, so it is a good idea to supplement the GPS and these directions with a good state highway map.

I have personally checked the coordinates for every site in this book. The GPS coordinates were checked against topographic maps and satellite photos, and they are correct. In addition, the road directions in the "**finding the site**" entries were verified. The directions were originally obtained by the way that I went to the site, and then verified using detailed mileages and directions from Google Maps.

I often found that the location information provided in other field guides or geologic publications was either incorrect, too vague, or purposely left out to keep collectors away. I have also included GPS coordinates for both the parking area and the site itself for the locations that merit both. In many cases the parking area is the same as the site. In some cases you have to park and then hike a significant distance to the site. I sometimes had to visit a site multiple times before I found the right location, and even then I was sometimes unsure if I had made it to the right spot. You may use this guide and in some cases find that the spot I recommended was not as good as an adjacent location, despite my efforts to find the best spot.

The site descriptions can be used to quickly provide information about a site so you will know what to expect during your visit. The **site type** refers to the type of occurrence, and this generally is a physical description of the site, which may be a streambed, roadcut, former quarry, or outcrop. The **land status** is based on the best available information and should let you know if you will be able to access the site without special permission or if you need to secure approval from a site owner for access. In many cases the official status of a parcel is not known, and these sites generally have access but no guarantee that they are actually open to visitors.

The **material** refers to the type of minerals, rocks, or fossils that a visitor would likely find of most interest. If they are listed, I can assure you that they are present at the site, but it still may take some effort to find them. In some cases if a mineral or fossil is reported to be present at a site but I did not find it, I have listed it as "reported" if the geologic conditions are appropriate for that mineral or fossil to be present. Just because I did not find it does not mean it is not there.

The **host rock** is the rock in which the material is found, and I have generally named the geologic formation or type of rock that best describes the enclosing rocks as the host rock. It is important to understand what rocks host your materials of interest, as you can use this knowledge to find similar sites.

The **difficulty** level is a guide to the likelihood of finding or observing the materials referenced in the site description. Some sites are loaded with material and you can step onto the site and find as much as you could possibly desire. Other sites take hours and hours of effort to find a single specimen, and even your most diligent efforts are not a guarantee that you will find or observe anything. If a site is marked as difficult, be aware that it may not be a good site for impatient collectors.

The **family-friendly** rating is very subjective and depends entirely on your family. If the description says yes without any qualifiers, you will generally find this to be a site where you can take small children and family members that can handle moderate walking and want to look at rocks. These sites also tend to be among the easier sites to find rocks. If the description says no, generally this is because the minerals or fossils are very hard to find, or because site access is very limited or difficult.

The **tools needed** field will let you know what kind of collecting tools you should bring to a site. In most cases a rock hammer and gloves are all that is needed, but for some sites you may be best served with a chisel, flat-bladed screwdriver, large sledgehammer, or shovel. At some sites, such as beach gravels, you may not need a hammer. I do not list standard safety equipment like boots, safety glasses, or hard hats here, as the emphasis is on tools. Unfortunately some sites do not allow collecting, so in these cases this field is simply "none." I usually bring my rock hammer, gloves, and day pack to virtually all sites, or at least keep all of them in reserve in the car if needed.

I have also included a section on **special concerns** so you know why this may not be a good site for everyone, especially if you are bringing small children, impatient collectors, friends, or family that may not appreciate the more adventurous aspects of rockhounding. This does not mean you should not take your family, but be prepared to deal with the issues mentioned in the site description.

As mentioned previously, do not assume that this guide gives you permission to collect or access the property. In general, all public sites in this guide can be accessed and you can look at the rocks, but many parks and government sites do not allow collecting or disturbing rocks. If the site is private, do not enter posted areas without obtaining permission, and be aware that some private grounds are not often clearly posted against trespassing. In many areas ownership and the rules regarding rock collecting are not clear, so if collecting regulations are unclear at any of these sites, leave your hammer in the car and simply enjoy looking at the rocks.

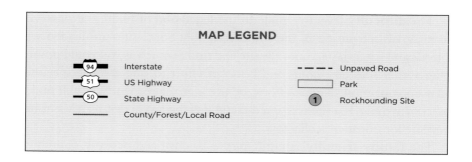

NOTES ON MAPS

Topographic maps are essential companions to the activities in this guide. Falcon has partnered with National Geographic to provide the best mapping resources. Each activity is accompanied by a detailed map and the name of the National Geographic TOPO! map (USGS), which can be downloaded for free from natgeomaps.com.

If the activity takes place on a National Geographic Trails Illustrated map, it will be noted. Continually setting the standard for accuracy, each Trails Illustrated topographic map is crafted in conjunction with local land managers and undergoes rigorous review and enhancement before being printed on waterproof, tear-resistant material. Trails Illustrated maps and information about their digital versions, which can be used on mobile GPS applications, can be found at natgeomaps.com.

EASTERN RIDGES AND LOWLANDS

1. Carol Beach Rocks

County: Kenosha
Site type: Lakeshore
Land status: Public Beach
Material: Various rounded beach rocks
Host rock: Unconsolidated beach sediments
Difficulty: Easy
Family-friendly: Yes
Tools needed: None
Special concerns: Proximity of water for nonswimmers
Special attractions: None
GPS parking: N42° 30.985' / W87° 48.667'
Topographic quadrangle: Kenosha, WI
Finding the site: From I-94, take exit 347 to WI 165, and head east toward Lake Michigan. Proceed about 6.6 miles and turn right (south) on Sheridan Road, which is the same as WI 32. Continue south about 1 mile, and turn left (east) onto 116th St. Go about 0.7 mile and turn north on Lakeshore Drive. Proceed for 0.6 mile and the parking area for Carol Beach will be on your right. You can walk directly to the beach from the parking area.

Rockhounding

This is a public beach with excellent access and lots of rocks. The rocks are generally small but represent the typical igneous, metamorphic, and sedimentary rocks of the Wisconsin side of Lake Michigan. I had hoped to find fossils in the rocks, but instead found that most of the Silurian dolostones of the area are largely devoid of fossils. Several large blocks of dolostone are used to protect the shoreline and I did not find any fossils or other minerals in these rocks, with the exception of some oxidized pyrite.

The rocks on the beach are not flat but are generally well rounded. The banding and colors come out with the constant rounding and polishing from the waves. Many of the granitic rocks have light blue quartz in a light orange feldspar matrix. Some of the granitic rocks are composed of deep orange feldspar. Many of the clastic sedimentary rocks show good layering and polishing. I also found several hematite-rich rocks with deep red and black bands. These undoubtedly originated from the iron-mining regions well to the north in the Upper Peninsula of Michigan and northern Wisconsin. I looked closely

The beach pebbles are generally well rounded.

Some of the granitic rocks have blue quartz and the sedimentary rocks have some distinct banding.

for agates and other decorative stones, but did not see any on this beach. This beach is very accessible and it is a good place to see the various stones that make their way onto Lake Michigan beaches.

References: Mudrey et al., 1982

2. Southport Park Beach Concrete

County: Kenosha
Site type: Lakeshore
Land status: Public Beach
Material: Rounded and slabs of concrete with aggregate
Host rock: Unconsolidated beach sediments
Difficulty: Easy
Family-friendly: Yes
Tools needed: None
Special concerns: Proximity of water for nonswimmers
Special attractions: None
GPS parking: N42° 33.750' / W87° 48.783'
GPS concrete on beach: N42º 33.783' / W87º 48.733'
Topographic quadrangle: Kenosha, WI
Finding the site: From I-94, take exit 344 to WI 50, which is 75th St. Proceed east for 7.1 miles. Turn right (south) on 2nd Ave, go 0.2 mile, and park in the parking area next to the park. Walk from here to Lake Michigan shoreline.

Rockhounding

This is another public beach but this has quite a bit more parking and it is likely more visited than Carol Beach to the south. This site has abundant Silurian dolostone blocks along the side of the beach to slow down erosion. I did not find any significant fossils in these rocks. What caught my eye at this site are the large rounded pieces of concrete. These apparently weathered from larger concrete blocks in the area and have been reworked extensively in the Lake Michigan surf.

The blocks resemble conglomerate and the aggregate in the concrete is uniformly spaced. Many of the aggregate pieces in the concrete are gray dolostone but some pieces have small fragments of granitic rocks and gneisses.

My father grew up in a house near Southport Beach. When I was about 9 or 10 we would go to this park in Lake Michigan when visiting my grandparents. I do not remember the rocks, but I remember that the beaches were covered with millions of dead alewives. Alewives are a type of small herring and were a major problem when their main predator, the Lake Trout, was nearly wiped out by sea lampreys. After the lampreys were brought under control, Pacific Salmon were introduced to the Great Lakes and helped to

The rocks are man-made but the aggregate in the matrix still forms an attractive pattern.

reduce the alewive population. Massive die offs of alewives were common in the 1960s and 1970s and still occur today, but not at the previous frequency or magnitude. I am sure many other rockhounds with ties to Lake Michigan remember these alewive die offs.

References: Mudrey et al., 1982

3. Racine Quarry Silurian Fossils

The fossiliferous areas are a short walk from the parking area.

County: Racine
Site type: Former Quarry, now Lake
Land status: Quarry Lake Park
Material: Silurian Fossils
Host rock: Racine Formation dolostone
Difficulty: Easy
Family-friendly: Yes
Tools needed: Hammer
Special concerns: Proximity of water for nonswimmers
Special attractions: Swimming and Fishing in Park
GPS parking: N42° 44.800' / W87° 49.250'
GPS fossils: N42° 44.867' / W87° 49.267'
Topographic quadrangle: Racine South, WI
Finding the site: From I-94, take exit 333 to WI 20 (Washington Avenue). Proceed about 5.3 miles east, and turn left (northeast) onto WI 31 (North Green Bay Road).

Crinoids are abundant in the Racine Formation dolostone at the collecting site.

Stay on North Green Bay Road for approximately 1.5 miles, and turn right (east) onto Northwestern Avenue. Continue about 0.3 mile and turn right (south) into Quarry Lake Park. Park in the parking lot near the beach and walk to the fossil-bearing rocks on the southeast end of the quarry.

Rockhounding

This site is a former quarry that dates back to the 1840s. It was first operated by the Horlick family, and the Horlick Lime and Stone Company was a major supplier of stone to rebuild Chicago after the Great Chicago Fire of 1871. Much of the stone from this quarry was donated to rebuild Chicago church buildings.

The quarry allowed the Horlick family to become active in other businesses. In 1873 the Horlicks formed a company to produce powered milk, which became known as malted milk. The product was developed to provide a healthy drink for infants. They dried malt, barley, and wheat into a powder and combined it with dehydrated milk. This was a highly digestible milk-based product that could be taken anywhere and stored for long periods

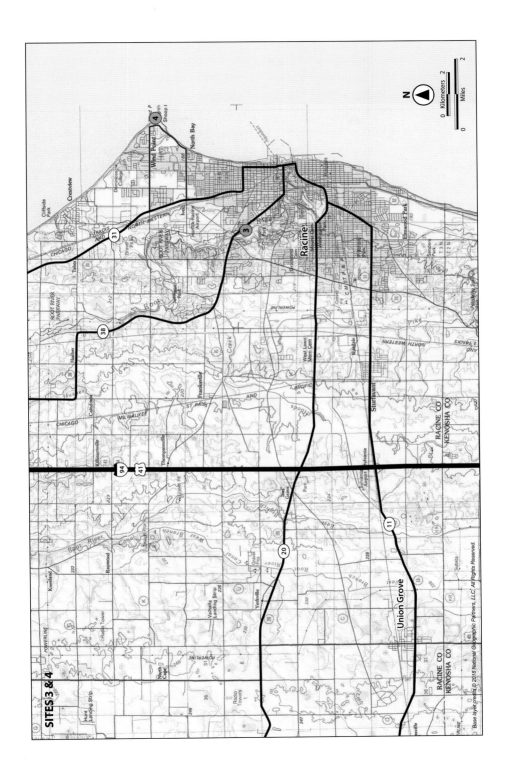

SITES 3 & 4

of time. It was used worldwide, and the Horlick Mountains in Antarctica were named after William Horlick by the polar explorer Richard Byrd for the Horlick's Malted Milk Company support of the Byrd Expedition to Antarctica in 1933–1935.

Like most nineteenth-century quarries along the Great Lakes, the site is vastly different that when it was operating. The quarry is now part of Quarry Lake Park, and it is accessible to the public. It is a large lake with a swimming beach, and it is located just east of the Root River in Racine.

The quarry extracted dolostone from the Silurian-age Racine Formation. When I visited the site in May 2017, the best fossils were found in the outcrops just north of the beach. It is a very easy area to walk to from the parking lot. The rocks have an abundance of crinoid fossils and the rock is extremely hard to break with a hammer. The best way to find the fossils is to look for loose pieces with weathered surfaces that expose fossils. I found several pieces with crinoid stems but did not see any other types of fossils. I also checked similar exposures on the west side of the lake, but I did not find any fossils here. The best place appears to be the area just north of the swimming beach, and this area shows the abundant broken rocks that indicate that many previous fossil collectors have been at this location.

The highwalls on the border of the lake are inaccessible unless you have a boat, and I do not recommend trying to extract rocks from the highwalls as loose rock can fall on you from above. Cliff diving is also prohibited at the park and anyone caught jumping off the cliffs is fined for trespassing. I met one of the managers of the park during my visit, and he was measuring the temperature of the water. He said it was still too cold for swimming, although it was late May. When I asked him about fossils he said that people are often looking for fossils in the park, and he gave no indication that fossil collecting was prohibited. The signs at the beach are primarily focused on stopping cliff divers and do not mention any restrictions to fossil collecting.

As I was leaving I also took a short hike to the Root River. This river appeared to be much lower in elevation than the quarry water level. The river had an abundance of similar rocks and it also appeared to have the potential for fossils, but the water level at the time of my visit prohibited a more detailed examination of the rocks. Collectors may also want to look at this area for fossils as well when visiting this park.

References: Evans, 2004; USGS, 2004; Wicklund, 2001; Mudrey et al., 1982

4. Wind Point Beach Silurian Fossils

Many of the best pieces with fossils are weathered and polished by wave action.

County: Racine
Site type: Public Beach
Land status: City Park
Material: Silurian Fossils
Host rock: Unconsolidated beach sediments
Difficulty: Easy
Family-friendly: Yes
Tools needed: None
Special concerns: Proximity of water for nonswimmers
Special attractions: Wind Point Lakehouse
GPS parking: N42° 46.883' / W87° 45.517'
GPS fossils on beach: N42° 44.867' / W87° 49.267'

Topographic quadrangle: Racine North, WI
Finding the site: From I-94, take exit 329, and proceed on Northeast Frontage Road to Four Mile Road. Turn east toward Lake Michigan, and proceed 9.8 miles. Four Mile Road then turns south and becomes Lighthouse Drive. Go 0.2 mile on Lighthouse Drive, and turn east onto Village Hall Drive. Follow this 0.1 mile to the parking area. Park here and walk to the beach.

Rockhounding

Wind Point is a point on the north end of Racine Harbor. It is known for the Wind Point Lighthouse, which is one of the tallest and oldest active lighthouses on the Great Lakes. The lighthouse was built in 1880 and is 108 feet high. It is open for tours and rentals.

A key feature of the Wind Point Lighthouse is that the park grounds are open daily and they offer parking and easy access to the shore of Lake Michigan. This area is pounded by waves, and the beach has loose rocks of Silurian dolostone as well as igneous and metamorphic rocks. White Silurian dolostone bedrock can be seen beneath the waves along the shoreline. The best place to find fossils is south of the grassy areas of the park where the shoreline is overgrown with brush.

While many of the dolostones are barren of fossils, several fossiliferous pieces can be found as you walk along the beach. I found pieces with abundant crinoids and brachiopods, and even found a piece with coral. A hammer is not necessary unless you want to trim pieces. Nearly all of the fossiliferous rocks are loose weathered dolostones and you have to spot these as you walk along the shore.

Unlike many Lake Michigan beaches, the shoreline at this locality is overgrown with brush so it is difficult to walk along the beach. Of course, this also means that fewer people are looking for fossils at this locality. This is also a relatively small stretch of shoreline so you should be able to check it out and find some interesting fossils soon after you start looking.

References: USGS, 2004; Sapulski, 2001

5. Estabrook Park Devonian Fossils

The Milwaukee River at Estabrook Park has one of the few Devonian exposures in Wisconsin.

County: Milwaukee
Site type: Outcrops along Milwaukee River
Land status: Estabrook Park
Material: Fossils and Pyrite
Host rock: Devonian Limestone
Difficulty: Easy
Family-friendly: Yes
Tools needed: Hammer and chisel
Special concerns: Area can be crowded during summer, must be discrete
Special attractions: Estabrook Beer Garden, right next to outcrops
GPS parking: N43° 06.050' / W87° 54.433'
GPS outcrops: N43° 05.967' / W87° 54.467'
Topographic quadrangle: Milwaukee, WI

This rock has a faint coral fossil on the right side.

Finding the site: From I-43, take exit 77A toward Hampton Avenue East. Use the middle lane to continue north onto Port Washington Rd, and then turn right (east) on Hampton Avenue East. Continue on Hampton Avenue East for 0.3 mile, and turn right (southeast) onto Estabrook Parkway. Continue about 0.4 mile and turn right (south) into the large parking lot on the south side of the Parkway. Park here and walk to the Milwaukee River. The Devonian outcrops are beneath a wooden walkway along the north bank of the river. The address of the park is 4600 Estabrook Pkwy, Milwaukee, WI 53217.

Rockhounding

Estabrook Park is one of the few accessible locations where Devonian rocks are exposed in southeastern Wisconsin. This is a popular park and it gets crowded in the summer, especially at the Estabrook Beer Garden. Fortunately the Beer Garden is right next to the fossils.

It is hard to believe that this park was also the site of a large cement manufacturing plant. The Milwaukee Cement Company operated a large cement quarrying and processing operation in what became the park from 1876 to 1914. The company produced natural cement from the limestones,

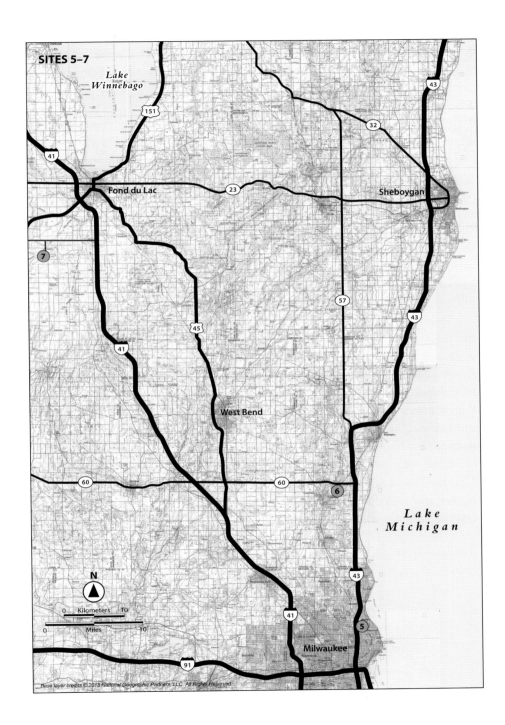

SITES 5–7

Lake
Winnebago

151

41

Fond du Lac   23   Sheboygan

32

43

7

45

41   57   43

West Bend

60   60   6

Lake
Michigan

N

0   Kilometers   10

0   Miles   10

43

41   5

91   Milwaukee

Base layer credits ©2018 National Geographic Partners, LLC. All Rights Reserved.

but the cement could not compete with cheaper Portland cement that could be made less expensively. When the cement company closed they left a landscape ravaged by mining and industrial operations. Eventually, the mining areas were filled in and the land was developed into a park by Milwaukee County.

I first came to Estabrook Park in 2003 to look for millerite. The only information I had was that it was located in outcrops along the Milwaukee River. I drove to the park and went to the first outcrops I could find, which were on the north bank of the river under a wooden walkway. I did not find any millerite, but I found carbonate rocks with vugs partially filled with a sticky dark brown to black substances that resembled tar.

I did not return to Estabrook Park until 2008 during a summer trip through Wisconsin. We visited the same outcrop, since this was the only location along the River with significant outcrops. We found more of the vuggy carbonates, but still no millerite. I had pretty much written this site off for millerite, but I was still intrigued by the carbonates with the tar.

In July of 2017 we came back to the site, but this time I wanted to check the shaly zones for fossils. During previous visits I was focused on the millerite and the strange vuggy rocks with the tar, and did not look hard for fossils. During this trip we found several coral fossils, some crinoids, and small brachiopods in the shaly zones of the outcrops. I also found more of the vuggy carbonates, and noticed that pyrite was also present in many of these carbonates. The pyrite is easy to spot as it often leaches in place and creates a rusty yellow zones.

I did not see any signs prohibiting rock collecting, but since this is a County Park I assume that collecting is not allowed. Even if you do not collect any rocks, it is worth checking out the fossils in the shaly limestone and the asphaltum–bearing dolomite.

References: Bagrowski, 1940; Swanson, 2015

6. Grafton Quarry Silurian Fossils

The former quarry highwalls are easy to see in the park.

County: Ozaukee
Site type: Former Quarry
Land status: Lime Kiln Park
Material: Silurian Fossils
Host rock: Silurian Dolostone
Difficulty: Difficult
Family-friendly: Yes
Tools needed: None
Special concerns: Must stay away from quarry highwalls
Special attractions: None
GPS parking: N43° 18.283' / W87° 57.500'
GPS outcrops: N43° 18.250' / W87° 57.500'
Topographic quadrangle: Cedarburg, WI
Finding the site: From I-43, take exit 92 and head west on Washington Street. Proceed about 0.7 mile and turn left (south) on Cheyenne Avenue. Continue

This dolostone is generally vuggy and both the crystals and fossils in the vugs are small.

0.7 mile and turn right (west) onto Falls Road. Continue 0.9 mile and turn left (south) onto South Green Bay Road. Go about 0.2 mile, and turn left (southwest) where South Green Bay Road continues into Lime Kiln Park. Continue another 0.3 mile and park in the parking area on the west side of the park. From here you can walk to the floor and slopes of the southern section of the former quarry.

Rockhounding

Lime Kiln Park is the site of a former quarry that produced lime from Silurian Dolostone. The quarry was operated by the Milwaukee Falls Lime Company, which was incorporated in 1890. It later was owned by the Tews Lime and Cement Company of Milwaukee. The plant had five kilns and burned cordwood for fuel. Lime was shipped from the quarry by rail.

Lime was a big industry at the start of the twentieth century. Nationally, Wisconsin ranked third in lime production. Pennsylvania was first, and Ohio second. Carbonate rocks throughout the nation were being quarried and burnt into lime for agriculture and construction. Lime was used to whitewash buildings and fences, as a soil conditioner, in the tanning industry, and for plaster and mortar. The dolostone also made good aggregate and crushed stone was used for roads.

However, Portland cement soon replaced mortar, and this was a key blow to lime producers. Industry consolidation, the rising cost of fuel, and reduced demand for agricultural lime resulted in the closing of the Lime Kiln Park operations in the 1920s. The Great Depression sealed the fate of many kilns nationwide and by the mid-twentieth century many lime kilns had long been closed. Lime production continued at many of the larger operations but the markets had changed significantly and operations were not coming back to this part of Grafton. Today, the quarry has been converted into a park, but three of the lime kilns have been preserved.

It is still possible to see some of the quarry rocks and look for fossils. Many of the Silurian quarries in the Milwaukee region were filled by dumps and construction debris when they closed, but the quarry at Lime Kiln Park still retains some of the highwalls and slopes.

The Lime Kiln park quarry is reportedly within a Silurian reef complex, and Silurian reefs often have an abundance of fossils such as corals and crinoids. I visited the site with my family in the summer of 2016. We parked at the parking area on the west side of the quarry. We then walked down a gentle slope to what I believe was the elevation of the former quarry floor along the west bank of the Milwaukee River. The highwalls are easy to see from this area. We hiked to the base of the highwalls and found a moderately steep trail going up the western highway. Much of this was overgrown with brush and it was difficult to walk or climb uphill in this area. Loose pieces of Silurian dolostone are abundant, but unfortunately we did not find many fossils. I found one small tiny coiled cephalopod, but that was about it. The dolostone is vuggy and I had hoped to find some calcite crystals in the vugs, but crystals were also absent.

However, when looking for fossils in a reef complex, you often have to look in many places. Some places are going to be barren while others may have abundant fossils. Although we did not find many fossils on this trip, this is a worthwhile place to check out as the access is excellent and the rocks are relatively well exposed and accessible. However, be very careful near the highwalls, as it is possible to fall off or get hit by rocks falling off the highwalls.

Reference: Harms, 1991

7. Oakfield Ledge Quarry Crystal Vugs

The quarry is cut right out of the dolomite.

County: Fond du Lac
Site type: Former Quarry
Land status: State Natural Area
Material: Quartz sunburst crystals in vugs
Host rock: Silurian Mayville Dolomite
Difficulty: Difficult
Family-friendly: Yes
Tools needed: None
Special concerns: No collecting, must stay away from quarry highwalls
Special attractions: None
GPS parking: N43° 40.450' / W88° 32.583'
GPS quarry: N43° 40.350' / W88° 33.467'
Topographic quadrangle: Oakfield, WI

Vugs in the dolomite can be seen in the quarry highwalls.

Finding the site: From I-41 south of Fond du Lac, take exit 95 and head west on US 151. Proceed about 2.6 miles west, and take the exit for CR-D. Head south on CR-D for 4.2 miles. Continue straight onto CR-B, and follow this for 0.9 mile. Turn left (south) onto Oak Street, which is a trunk to CR-Y. Proceed 0.4 mile. The public parking area and trailhead to the quarry will be on your right. Park here, and follow the trail to the quarry.

Rockhounding

This abandoned quarry near Oakfield is within the Oakfield Ledge. This is a long section of the Niagara Escarpment in Wisconsin. This ridge is nearly 650 miles long and goes from Waukesha County and forms the backbone of the Door Peninsula. It then curves in a broad arc through Ontario and ends at Niagara Falls in New York. The escarpment near Oakfield is known as "the ledge" as it forms prominent cliffs of rock that are nearly 40 feet high. The town of Oakfield originally considered the name "Lime" since quarrying along the Ledge was a major industry for the region. However, fractures in the Ledge eroded into deep crevices, and the forested areas along the ledge had many oak trees, so the town took the name Oakfield.

Some of the vugs have small radiating crystals of quartz.

The Wisconsin Department of Natural Resources purchased this section of the Oakfield Ledge, and it became a State Natural Area in 1983. Unfortunately, while the area has been preserved for public access, no collecting of plants, fossils, or minerals is allowed in this area. It still is a worthwhile quarry to visit, as the rocks are well exposed and crystals can be found in some of the rocks on the quarry floor.

I visited the area in May 2017. The parking area is large and can accommodate several vehicles. I followed the trail from the parking lot, and this was flat and an easy hike. Several wind turbines are prominent to the east and south, which is an indication of the strong winds that blow across the top of the Ledge. My hike was approximately 25 minutes, and I was stunned when I arrived at the quarry. From the satellite photos I thought this was a small quarry. Instead, I found that it was a massive long, wide quarry that carved out millions of tons of dolomite. The highwalls were nearly 30 feet high. The trail goes right up to edge, so you have to be very careful when approaching the quarry. You definitely do not want to be walking and texting or looking at your maps app as it would be easy to walk off the highwall.

I was not sure how to get down into the quarry, but I saw trash and signs of a fire pit, so I knew there had to be a way. I walked south along the east side and found a trail that followed the western side of the quarry to the quarry floor. Once I was inside the quarry it no longer looked as big. I have noticed this phenomenon before in several mines I had visited. They look large and intimidating when you first see them, but once you are in the pit they no longer seem as big.

I had heard that fossils were in some of the quarries near Oakfield, and I looked for indications of fossils. The rocks in the quarry are a vuggy dolomite, and I did not see any fossils. However, when I looked in the vugs, I saw many with fine druzy quartz crystals. I later found some vuggy dolomite with starburst quartz crystals within the vugs. These starburst crystals were only about ¼ inch in diameter, but they were numerous. They were white quartz, and this contrasted nicely with the light gray to light tan of the dolostone.

The crystals are not abundant and it takes some effort to find the rocks with starburst crystals in the vugs. The best way to see them is to look at previous broken rocks on the quarry floor and near the highwalls. Look for the vuggy rocks and check for crystals. If they are present you should be able to see them easily. However, be extremely careful near the highwalls. Falling is a risk, but falling rock may be a greater risk.

References: Dott and Attig, 2004

8. Wequiock Falls Ordovician Fossils

This slab with fossils was found in the creek.

County: Brown
Site type: Stream bed
Land status: Wequiock County Park
Material: Fossils
Host rock: Ordovician
Difficulty: Easy
Family-friendly: Yes
Tools needed: None, just a hammer for trimming.
Special concerns: County Park, not sure of collecting status
Special attractions: Green Bay Packers Hall of Fame
GPS parking: N44º 34.083' / W87º 52.767'
GPS site: N44º 34.150' / W87º 52.833'
Topographic quadrangle: Green Bay East, WI
Finding the site: From Green Bay, take I-43 southeast to exit 185. Merge onto WI 57, and continue 7.1 miles to Van Lanen Road, and turn left (west). Continue about 0.1 mile, and make a sharp turn onto a narrow paved but unnamed road. This road leads to the parking area for the park. This parking area is less than 0.1 mile from

Van Lanen Road. Park here, and walk to the bridge next to Bay Settlement Road. Follow the stairs near the bridge to the creek bed, and walk upstream to the falls or downstream to the fossil area.

Rockhounding

This is an easily accessed site that is a great stop when in nearby Green Bay or when taking a trip up the Door County peninsula. We visited the site in July 2016. The parking lot for Wequiock County Park had plenty of parking space available. From the parking area we walked to a bridge that crossed the creek in the park. Although this creek is unnamed on the topographic map, this is Wequiock Creek, based on information from the Brown County website. The creek drains into Lake Michigan, which is approximately 1 mile to the west.

We first walked southwestward upstream to the waterfall that formed along the Niagara Escarpment. This is a prominent feature of eastern Wisconsin geology. The escarpment formed from a capstone of early Silurian dolomites that overlie softer Ordovician shales. At Wequiock Park, the resistant rock that forms the lip of the waterfall is the early Silurian Maysville Dolomite. This is a dolomite that is light gray, medium to thick bedded dolomite with chert nodules. This is underlain by the softer late Ordovician Maquoketa Formation. This is shale with argillaceous dolomite.

Since this was July there was very little water in the creek, and there was almost no water coming over the waterfall. The area was crowded with other families visiting the falls. We started looking for fossils around the falls and I was disappointed that we did not find any. A couple of small children found some small horn corals in the creek, and while they were quite excited I knew there had to be more fossils in the area, based on the online descriptions of the area.

We then went away from the crowds by heading downstream through a tunnel. When we emerged at the other side we found that the creek had widened but the sides were still fairly steep. I soon found several large rocks with abundant brachiopods, bryozoans, and horn corals. These are best described as a fossil "hash" as they are a jumbled mass of fossils with little or no order or bedding.

The key to this site is to focus your efforts in the area downstream of the tunnel. I also found several loose pieces of horn corals in the creek. A hammer is not really needed unless you want to trim specimens.

References: Dutch, 2013; Sivon, 1980

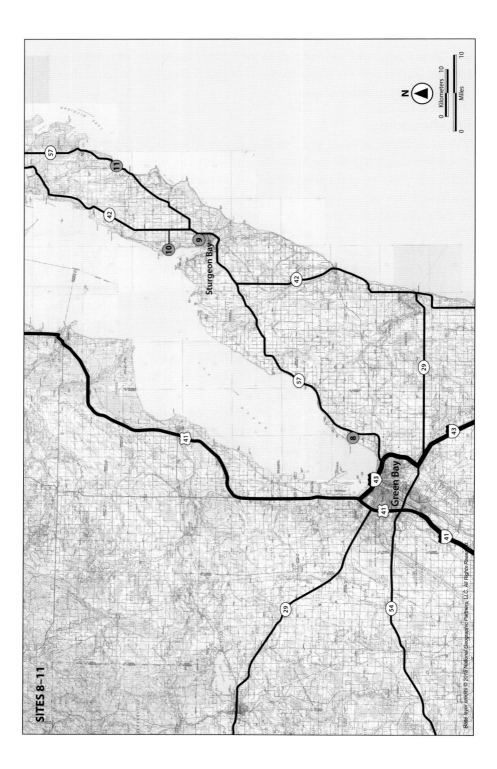

SITES 8-11

N

0 Kilometers 10
0 Miles 10

LAKE MICHIGAN

57

11

42

10

9

Sturgeon Bay

42

57

41

8

29

43

Green Bay

43

41

41

29

54

Base layer credits © 2018 National Geographic Partners, LLC. All Rights Reserved.

9. Sturgeon Bay Silurian Coral Fossils

County: Door
Site type: Outcrops
Land status: Private, but not posted
Material: Fossils
Host rock: Silurian Dolomite
Difficulty: Easy
Family-friendly: Yes
Tools needed: None, no hammering allowed
Special concerns: Wal-Mart parking lot, be mindful of traffic
Special attractions: Potawatomi and Whitefish Dunes State Parks
GPS outcrops: N44º 51.133' / W87º 21.467'
Topographic quadrangle: Sturgeon Bay East, WI
Finding the site: From Green Bay, take WI 57/42 to Sturgeon Bay. After you cross the Bridge over Sturgeon Bay, continue 3.1 miles to a traffic circle and take the second exit to the west, which is Egg Harbor Road/WI Business 42. Proceed 0.7 mile west, and turn north into the Wal-Mart Supercenter parking lot. Park on the east side of the parking lot. The outcrops are on the east side of the parking lot and north and east sides of the store. The address of the Wal-Mart is 1536 Egg Harbor Road, Sturgeon Bay, WI 54235.

Rockhounding

Land development usually obscures or obliterates fossil and mineral localities, but in many cases the excavations needed for building new stores and parking lots can provide great exposures to see rocks. This is especially true in Door County, which is generally flat except for exposures along the Silurian escarpment.

The Wal-Mart Supercenter was constructed on the southern slope of a broad high area, and consequently a lot of rock had to be excavated to make a flat area for the store. This resulted in some excellent exposures of Silurian dolomite along the eastern and northern sides of the store.

During a trip through Door County we stopped at the Supercenter to load up on supplies, which included food and new swimsuits. While my son and daughter were shopping I had the opportunity to observe the outcrops

The outcrops are immediately east of the parking lot.

next to the parking lot. This area is not posted and I did not use a hammer, and focused on looking for loose fossils and fossils in the outcrop.

I hoped to see lots of fossils immediately, but I found that most of the outcrop next to the parking lot was barren. However, with some effort I soon found some coral fossils. The corals fossils are mainly *Favosites*, which are

This piece has a coral fossil exposed on its surface.

distinguished by a hexagonal pattern that resembles a honeycomb. *Favosites* is an extinct genus of coral and is common in the Silurian dolomites in eastern Wisconsin.

I stayed close to my car and limited my observations to the parking lot outcrops next to the customer parking lot. Further north the exposures are much larger as a large amount of rocks had to be removed for construction of the store. I did not ask for permission to hunt in this area due to limitations on our time, and I thought that obtaining permission from a store manager to look for fossils would be all but impossible. Fortunately, it was still possible to find several sections of the outcrop that had fossils. In terms of access this place is hard to beat, but I highly recommend being watchful for Wal-Mart security and refrain from using a hammer at this site.

References: Thwaites and Lentz, 1922

10. Sturgeon Bay Quarry Park Silurian Fossils

County: Door
Site type: Former quarry and stone piers
Land status: George K. Pinney County Park
Material: Silurian Corals and Brachiopods
Host rock: Silurian Dolomite
Difficulty: Easy
Family-friendly: Yes
Tools needed: None, no hammering allowed
Special concerns: Quarry highwall, slipping on rocks
Special attractions: Fishing on piers
GPS parking: N44° 51.133' / W87° 21.467'
Topographic quadrangle: Idlewild, WI
Finding the site: From Green Bay, take WI 57/42 to Sturgeon Bay. As you approach Sturgeon Bay, turn left (north) on South Neenah Avenue, and go 0.6 mile. Turn right (northeast) onto Oregon Street, and go 0.3 mile. Then turn left (northwest) on South 1st Ave, and stay on this for 0.6 mile. Then turn left (north) onto North 3rd Ave, and continue 0.8 mile, and this then turns into Bay Shore Dr. Continue north on Bay Shore. Drive for 4.3 miles to parking at the George K. Pinney Park. You can park next to the quarry or Sturgeon Bay.

Rockhounding

This is a County Park that was made next to a large quarry. Google Maps indicates this as the George K. Pinney County Park, but it is also known locally as Olde Stone Quarry County Park. According to the historical marker at the park, John Leathem and Thomas Smith established this dolomite quarry at the mouth of Sturgeon Bay in 1893. They produced dimension stone for building harbors around Lake Michigan. The quarry became a major operation when it began to supply crushed stone for roads, railroad beds, and concrete. In 1914, a huge stone crushing plant was constructed on the lower quarry floor. On the upper level, a steam shovel loaded stone into carts, which were hauled to the crushing plant by a quarry locomotive. Conveyors carried the crushed stone to screens where it was washed and sorted. From stockpiles, the stone was loaded onto ships converted to barges. The steel frontage and

The main pier on the northwest side of the park has large boulders and rocks with Silurian fossils.

wooden pilings along the shore are remnants of the quarry dock. The crushing plant, rail line, and conveyors are all long gone.

Unfortunately, the upper floors of the quarry remain on private property, and cannot be accessed from the park. Both the north and south ends of the parking lot near the highwall are marked as private property. The lower floor highwall is well exposed and there are abundant loose rocks along this highwall. We did not see any restrictions to going near the highwall or any signs prohibiting fossil collecting, but since this is a county park it is reasonable to assume that collecting is not encouraged and may be prohibited. We looked for fossils in these rocks, and despite our efforts only found one small coral fossil next to the highwalls. I had anticipated that Silurian corals and brachiopods would be abundant in these rocks.

However, the piers that extend into Sturgeon Bay are made of large boulders and rocks that are almost certainly from this quarry as well. I walked onto the main pier on the northwest side of the park, and looked closely at the rocks. Almost immediately I saw many rocks that had brachiopods

Silurian brachiopods are the most common fossil on the pier, but you can also see coral fossils in the boulders and rocks.

and corals. Many of the rocks do not have fossils but with a little effort you can find brachiopods and corals easily. The boulders have several sections with coral fossils, and some of the smaller rocks have both brachiopods and corals.

References: Thwaites and Lentz, 1922; Wisconsin Historical Markers, 2012

11. Kangaroo Lake Wayside Park Silurian Fossils

This coral fossil with the hexagonal patterns was found loose on the outcrops at the wayside.

County: Door
Site type: Roadside park
Land status: Uncertain, may be part of local county park
Material: Silurian Corals
Host rock: Silurian Dolomite
Difficulty: Hard
Family-friendly: Yes
Tools needed: None, no hammering allowed
Special concerns: Mosquitoes, ticks
Special attractions: Cave Point County Park and Whitefish Dunes State Park
GPS parking: N45° 00.267' / W87° 09.933'
Topographic quadrangle: Baileys Harbor West, WI

Finding the site: From the intersection of Clay Banks Road and WI 57 in Sturgeon Bay, proceed 17.5 miles north on WI 57. The outcrops are at a wayside park located about 2,000 feet north of the intersection of WI 57 and Logerquist Road. Park at the wayside, and the outcrops are next to the parking area.

Rockhounding

This site is not on Kangaroo Lake but is just south of the Lake. I had heard that fossils could be found on the shores of Kangaroo Lake, but unfortunately the areas that I tried to look at were private. However, these outcrops at this roadside park appear to be on public land.

The outcrops have nearly horizontal beds and are weathered and covered in many places with moss. Fossils are not abundant and it is challenging to find fossils here. However, I found an interesting coral fossil lying on one of the bedding surfaces. It was discolored with dirt and moss but it consisted almost entirely of hexagonal plates that are indicative of coral. Unfortunately it was the only one that I found, but where there is one there are often more. There is also a small trail that leads west into the woods, and some additional outcrops are in these woods. We did not find any fossils here but I did come across a small piece of dolomite with vugs lined with small clear quartz crystals.

This site also has a small plaque that marks the 45th degree parallel line of latitude, which is exactly halfway between the North Pole and the Equator. This was interesting but on reading the plaque it notes that the 45th parallel is actually one-half mile south of the wayside. This is nice information, but usually the plaque goes at the spot, not as a reference to a spot that is not really close to the plaque.

References: Thwaites and Lentz, 1922

WESTERN UPLAND

12. Janesville Ordovician Fossils

The fossils are found in the shaly rocks and include crinoids and bryozoans.

County: Rock
Site type: Roadcut
Land status: Road right-of-way, next to Rockport Park
Material: Ordovician Fossils
Host rock: Sandstone and limestone of Ordovician Ancell Group
Difficulty: Moderately difficult
Family-friendly: Yes
Tools needed: None
Special concerns: Traffic, uncertain of collecting status
Special attractions: Fishing in Rock River
GPS parking: N42° 39.983' / W89° 03.117'
GPS fossils: N42° 40.133' / W89° 03.067'
Topographic quadrangle: Janesville West, WI
Finding the site: From WI 11 west of Janesville, take the exit to Afton Road. Proceed northeast for 2.2 miles to the Bellrichard Bridge, and park in this area. Go to the first road east of the bridge and walk north. The outcrops are exposed on the east side of the small ridge that is on the west side of this road.

The fossils are found in the northern section of this roadcut.

Rockhounding

This site has Ordovician fossils in a tan sandy limestone. The fossils are mainly crinoids and some bryozoans. The site is easy to reach by a short walk from the parking area just west of the Bellrichard Bridge.

When I first reviewed this site I was frustrated as the rocks appeared to be barren of fossils. I started near the south end of the outcrop and worked by way north. The rocks are bedded and are nearly horizontal, and much of the outcrops are covered with brush and grass. I finally found fossils near the north end of the outcrop. The fossils were relatively small and were mainly crinoids and bryozoans.

There are some additional rocks exposed along the Rock River, but I did not find any fossils in these rocks. Although there are many quarries in the area they are on private land. This site, while it does not have an abundance of fossils, is easy to access, and with some persistence you should be able to find some fossils.

Reference: USGS, 2004

SITES 12–16

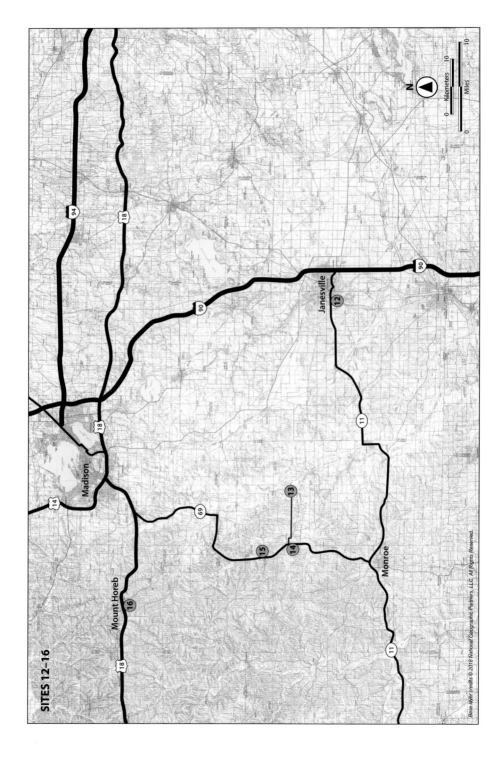

13. Albany Glauconitic Sandstone

County: Green
Site type: Roadcut
Land status: Likely highway right-of-way, not posted
Material: Green glauconitic sandstone
Host rock: Sandstone of Ordovician Ancell Group
Difficulty: Easy
Family-friendly: Yes
Tools needed: Hammer
Special concerns: Traffic
Special attractions: None
GPS parking: N42° 44.450' / W89° 28.950'
Topographic quadrangle: Albany, WI
Finding the site: From the intersection of WI 59 and CR-E in Albany, go north on CR-E for 1.2 miles. Turn left (west) onto CH-EE. Follow this for 3.0 mile. Look for a prominent outcrop with green sandstone on the north side of the CH-EE. Parking is available on the shoulder on the south side of the road.

Rockhounding

This is a colorful outcrop that we noticed when driving from eastern Wisconsin to the lead–zinc mining districts of southwestern Wisconsin. The cliffs are primarily sandstone with a distinct light green bed of sandstone that is approximately 4 feet thick exposed in the hillside. The outcrop is too high to reach safely by climbing, but many pieces have fallen to the base of the cut. The green sandstone and the light tan sandstone below it are relatively soft and easily eroded. They are capped by a more resistant formation that forms the top of the hillside, and this protects the lower sandstone from eroding away.

The green is likely due to glauconite. Glauconite is an iron potassium phyllosilicate and is characterized by its green color and low resistance to weathering. It is an authigenic mineral, which means that it formed after the rocks were deposited. It forms in low oxygen environments associated with continental shelf marine deposition with slow rates of deposition. It is a common mineral in the Cambrian and early Paleozoic sediments of southern and central Wisconsin, but it is often weathered to a dark gray or found in highly friable sandstones that are difficult to pick up without crumbling to pieces.

The glauconitic sandstone is a distinct green and pieces are at the base of the roadcut.

If the green mineral is not glauconite, the color is likely due to some type of green clay or chlorite. I did not have the benefit of further testing, such as x-ray diffraction or other methods, to confirm that it is glauconite, but that is largely irrelevant when you are mainly looking for interesting rocks that stand out from others. This is a colorful rock and the outcrop is well worth a visit when in southern Wisconsin.

Reference: USGS, 2004

14. Monticello Sandstone

The sandstone is exposed on both sides of WI 69.

County: Green
Site type: Roadcuts
Land status: Highway right-of-way
Material: Ordovician sandstone
Host rock: Ordovician Ancell Group sandstone
Difficulty: Easy
Family-friendly: Yes
Tools needed: Hammer
Special concerns: Traffic on WI 69
Special attractions: None
GPS parking: N42° 44.450' / W89° 28.950'
Topographic quadrangle: Monticello, WI
Finding the site: From intersection of CR-C and WI 69 at Monticello, proceed about 600 feet south. The sandstone is exposed in large roadcuts on both sides of WI 69. Parking is available on the shoulder on the west side of WI 69.

This piece shows some of the limonite banding in this rock.

Rockhounding

This is an interesting locality as it exposes a fine- to medium- grained quartz sandstone. The sandstone is relatively soft and it is easy to obtain large pieces. Some of the sandstone has bands of iron staining, and cross beds can be seen in parts of the roadcut.

Most of the sandstone is soft and crumbles when hit by a hammer. The sandstone does not contain fossils, and some of the section is monotonous as it is all fine- to medium-grained sand. The USGS described the Ancell Group as primarily orthoquartzitic sand stone with minor limestone, shale, and conglomerate, but at this section it is entirely sandstone. The Ancell Group includes the Glenwood and St. Peter Formations.

I was able to find large pieces of orange and white sandstone, and since it is so close to the car you do not have to carry it for any significant distance. Since it is so soft it is easy to trim to whatever size you would like. However, it will invariably get smaller with time if you leave it outside and exposed to rain. At least it is a relatively pure sandstone and does not have pyrite or other metallic minerals that can leach into the ground.

Reference: USGS, 2004

15. New Glarus Fossils

A fragment of a small brachiopod can been seen left of the hammer.

County: Green
Site type: Roadcuts
Land status: Highway right-of-way
Material: Ordovician fossils
Host rock: Ordovician Sinnippee Group limestone and dolostone
Difficulty: Difficult
Family-friendly: No, too much traffic
Tools needed: Hammer
Special concerns: Traffic on WI 69
Special attractions: New Glarus Brewery
GPS parking: N42° 47.167' / W89° 37.683'
Topographic quadrangle: New Glarus, WI
Finding the site: From New Glarus, take WI 69 south. Turn right (west) onto CR-NN, which leads to New Glarus Woods State Park. Park at the shoulder on the

south side of CR-NN on the east side of WI 69. The roadcuts are to the north on both sides of WI 69.

Rockhounding

The rocks at this locality are fossil-bearing roadcuts of Ordovician Sinnippee Group limestones and dolomites. The hillside slopes to the highway, and the rocks are covered with soil and thick plant growth. The exposures are best seen in the upper sections of the slope of the roadcut.

I found this locality through a fossil listing for Wisconsin sites by Kenney (2016). This is an interesting database and it also lists fossils for other states as well. The listing described a locality for Ordovician fossils on WI 69 at New Glarus, and I used topographic maps and satellite images on Google Maps to find the most likely location for the roadcut. The most prominent roadcut was just north of the intersection of CR-NN and WI 69 on the west side of WI 69.

Fortunately there is a good shoulder to park at on the south side of CR-NN, and you can walk directly to the exposures on the sides of WI 69. I visited the site in May of 2017 and the area was thick with vegetation and with ticks. The best way to find the fossils is to walk along the base of the outcrop and look for loose rocks. The fossils are generally quite small and a sharp eye is needed to see the fossils.

The rocks are exposed on both sides of WI 60, but all the fossiliferous rocks that I found were limited to the west side of the highway. Due to the traffic I also highly recommend wearing a high-visibility vest.

References: Kenney, 2016; USGS, 2004

16. Mount Horeb Fossils

The roadcuts are exposed along a long stretch of US 151.

County: Dane
Site type: Roadcuts
Land status: Highway right-of-way
Material: Ordovician fossils
Host rock: Ordovician Sinnippee Group limestone, dolostone, and shale
Difficulty: Difficult
Family-friendly: No, too much traffic
Tools needed: Hammer
Special concerns: Traffic is heavy on US 151
Special attractions: Cave of the Mounds
GPS parking beneath CR-JG Bridge: N42° 59.650' / W89° 43.833'
GPS parking at northeast ramp at exit 65: N43° 00.083' / W89° 45.517'
Topographic quadrangle: Mt. Vernon, WI
Finding the site: From Madison, take US 18 west, and this turns into US 151.
This is a very broad four lane highway. South of Mt. Horeb you will see that both

This piece has a cast of a spiral creature.

sides of the highway have long continuous roadcuts. From exit 69, continue west on US 151 about 1.8 miles to a bridge that crosses the highway. This is the CR-JG Bridge. You can park under this bridge on the north side of the highway, and outcrops with fossils are at this area. Another parking area near the roadcut is approximately 1.5 miles west on the north side of the exit ramp for exit 65 to Business Route US 18.

Rockhounding

This is a very long roadcut on both sides of US 151 south of Mount Horeb. Although it is long, it is challenging to find a safe location for parking to observe the outcrops. The roadcut appears similar throughout the area and fossils can likely be found throughout the roadcut.

The rocks are limestones, dolostones, and shales of the Ordovician Sinnippee Group. The fossils are generally small and can be hard to find. It is best to find the fossils in loose rocks along the base of the roadcut.

I was initially frustrated at this roadcut as I had hoped the fossils would be more abundant. Like many fossil localities, it depends on the part of the

Small fragments of brachiopods can be seen on many of the rocks in this exposure.

section where you look. I kept my eyes on the ground and the rocks for signs of fossils. I soon found brachiopod fragments, and these are easy to spot in the rocks. I also found the spiral cast of what appeared to be a small gastropod.

The first place that I stopped was beneath the bridge for CR-JG. While parking here is adequate I did not like this area as I am always concerned that my parked car may get unwanted attention from the highway patrol. I soon left this spot and drove to the next exit, which was approximately 1.5 miles west. The exit ramp had a long exposure of similar rocks, and I found a safe parking area along this ramp.

The roadcut had fossils in this area as well, and I also noticed several beds with nodules of chert. Most of this chert was gray, but some of it had an orange tint. This chert was easy to break out of the roadcut with the pick end of my hammer. If you collect at this site, make sure that you also look at some of the chert exposed in the roadcuts.

References: Nehm and Bemis, 2002

17. Mineral Point White Sandstone

The white sandstone is right at road level.

County: Iowa
Site type: Roadcut
Land status: Likely highway right-of-way, not posted
Material: White Sandstone
Host rock: Ordovician St. Peter Sandstone
Difficulty: Easy
Family-friendly: Yes
Tools needed: Hammer
Special concerns: Traffic
Special attractions: None
GPS parking: N42° 52.483' / W90° 12.400'
Topographic quadrangle: Mineral Point, WI
Finding the site: From the intersection of Ridge Street and WI 23 in Mineral Point, take WI 39 1.7 miles west. The outcrops are exposed on the west side of WI 39. Park on the shoulder of the road, but make sure to pull off to a safe location.

The sandstone is nearly all quartz except for some minor iron staining.

Rockhounding

This outcrop is an excellent, easy-to-reach location of St. Peter Sandstone. It is a white, fine-grained Ordovician sandstone that is almost entirely quartz. Much of the sandstone is friable and crumbles easily, but some large chunks that are reasonably intact can be found at this exposure. In addition to the white sandstone, the locality has some sandstone with orange iron-stained bands. Some of the sandstone with the orange banding is better cemented and not as friable.

References: Batten and Attig, 2010

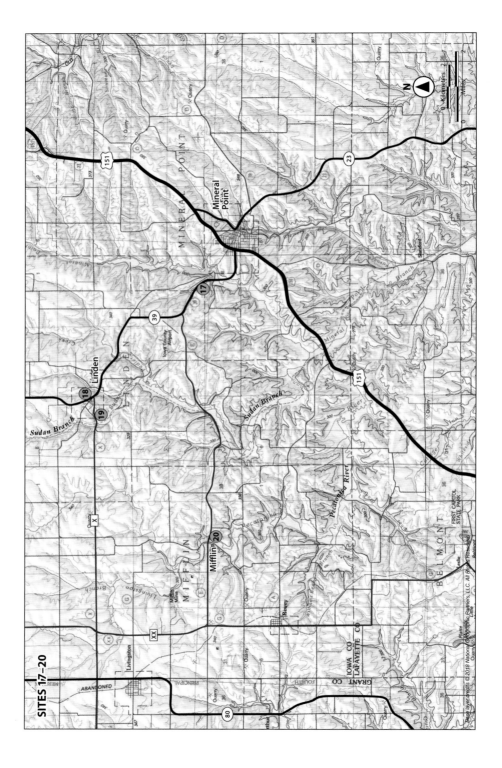

SITES 17–20

18. Linden Lead Mine Calcite and Sphalerite

Hand-sized pieces of calcite can be found on the ground around the mine.

County: Iowa
Site type: Former lead mine site
Land status: Uncertain, not posted
Material: Calcite, sphalerite, galena
Host rock: Ordovician Galena Formation dolomitic limestone
Difficulty: Easy
Family-friendly: Yes
Tools needed: Hammer
Special concerns: Land status uncertain
Special attractions: None
GPS parking: N42° 55.200' / W90° 16.250'
Topographic quadrangle: Linden, WI

There is an abundance of rocks on the mine dumps.

Finding the site: Assuming you are approaching Linden from the south on WI 39, come to Linden, and near the center of town stay on WI 39 as it forks to the right and goes north. Continue about 500 feet, and turn right (east) onto Valley Street. Continue another 500 feet to the intersection with Wisconsin Street. Here the streets meet at a corner. At this corner you will see a gate. The former mine area and dump material are in this gate area and it is surrounded by a fence.

Rockhounding

This is a former lead mine, based on the label "Lead Mine" on the topographic quadrangle for the area. I do not know the name of this mine, so I am simply referring to it as the Linden Lead Mine. At the time we visited the site the gate was open, and it was apparent that the area was well trafficked. It appeared to be some type of municipal site for getting rock fill, but getting fill from a former lead mine is certainly not a good idea. The area was open and not posted, so we drove to the large piles. This was on a late weekday afternoon, and none of the neighbors showed the slightest interest in our entering the site.

This dense rock has calcite and bands of sphalerite.

The piles are several hundred tons of mine waste rock, and consist mainly of large and small pieces of Galena Formation dolomite. Many of the rocks are not mineralized but it is easy to find pieces with white calcite and dark brown sphalerite. I believe that I found some galena but it was difficult to confirm due to the fine grain size and weathering in the rocks. The best pieces, like in most metal mines, are very dense and loaded with sphalerite and calcite. The best way to find pieces of white calcite was to look on the ground for bright white patches. These are often the tips of larger pieces that have been run over by cars and trucks.

References: Batten and Attig, 2010

19. Linden Pyrite and Chalcopyrite

Pieces of white calcite can also be found among these rocks.

County: Iowa
Site type: Rock pile in drainage
Land status: Uncertain, not posted, may be city land
Material: Pyrite, chalcopyrite, calcite
Host rock: Ordovician Galena Formation dolomitic limestone
Difficulty: Easy
Family-friendly: Yes
Tools needed: Hammer
Special concerns: Land status uncertain
Special attractions: None
GPS parking: N42° 55.000' / W90° 16.867'
Topographic quadrangle: Linden, WI
Finding the site: The site is at the corner of Babcock and Galena Streets in Linden. Take WI 39 through Linden, and stay to the left when WI 39 forks to the right.

Continue about 800 feet on Main Street, and turn left (southwest) onto Babcock Street. Continue 0.3 mile to the intersection with Galena Street. There is a small pumping station that may be for the local sewer system. There is space for one car and this is undoubtedly used for those serving this station.

Rockhounding

I found this site through the use of Google Maps. I have found that many public projects in former mining districts that need rocks for bank stabilization or similar projects go for the cheapest rocks available. In a mining district, what can be cheaper than mine dump rocks?

In this case I was correct, as the rocks used for the drainage at this pumping station are full of pyrite, chalcopyrite, and calcite. They undoubtedly came from a former mine site. I think there may also be some sphalerite and galena at this site but I focused on the larger pieces with pyrite and chalcopyrite.

Most of the best rocks are right next to the broken asphalt near the station. The mineralized rocks are easy to spot as they are generally dark brown, dense, and have weathered and fresh pyrite on their surfaces. Cracking these open often reveals large vugs that are filled with pyrite and chalcopyrite crystals.

References: Batten and Attig, 2010

20. Mifflin Ordovician Fossils

The fossils are found in the shaly sections of the roadcut.

County: Iowa
Site type: Roadcut
Land status: Uncertain, not posted
Material: Ordovician crinoids, brachiopods, bryozoans
Host rock: Ordovician Platteville Formation dolomite
Difficulty: Easy
Family-friendly: Yes
Tools needed: Hammer
Special concerns: Limited parking
Special attractions: Pecontanica River Woods State Natural Area
GPS parking: N42° 52.250' / W90° 20.917'
Topographic quadrangle: Mifflin, WI
Finding the site: From the intersection of Ridge Street and WI 39 in Mineral Point, take WI 39 west 2.7 miles, and turn left (west) onto CR-E. Continue on CR-E for

6.8 miles. Just before you reach the small town of Mifflin the outcrops will be on the right (north) side of CR-E. Park just before the guard rail near the outcrops. Parking is limited, and you must be careful to pull far enough off the road to avoid traffic.

Rockhounding

This is a relatively new roadcut that has been made at this site. A review of satellite photographs from Google Maps show that the road was previously much narrower. CR-E has been widened and the stormwater channel for drainage into the Pecontonica River has also been deepened. This has made this roadcut much larger and exposed many more rocks.

The rocks are within the Ordovician Platteville Formation, which is part of the Sinnipee Group. The Platteville Formation is fine-grained light gray dolomite, and some sections are fossiliferous. At this location the bedding is nearly horizontal and the dolomite ranges from gray to light tan. Most of the gray dolomite is barren of fossils, and the tan rocks are the ones that have most of the fossils. The best way to find the fossils is to look for the brown, thin-bedded sections of the dolomite that have broken off the outcrop. The weathered surfaces sometimes contain fossils. The fossils include crinoids, brachiopods, and bryozoans. The fossils here are not as abundant as at some localities, but this is an exposure that is worth checking out. It is a relatively new roadcut and may not have been visited by many fossil collectors.

References: Batten and Attig, 2010

21. Shullsburg Chert

The bedding in the Ordovician rocks is nearly horizontal.

County: Lafayette
Site type: Roadcut
Land status: Highway right-of-way
Material: Ordovician limestone and dolostone
Host rock: Ordovician Sinnippee Group limestone and dolostone
Difficulty: Easy
Family-friendly: No, too close to road
Tools needed: Hammer
Special concerns: Traffic on WI 11
Special attractions: Badger Mining Museum
GPS parking: N42° 34.000' / W90° 16.200'
Topographic quadrangle: New Diggings, WI-IL
Finding the site: From the intersection of CR-O and WI 11 in Shullsburg, proceed west approximately 1.9 miles on WI 11. Park on the north side of WI 11 on the shoulder just east of the roadcuts. The roadcuts are exposed on both sides of WI 11.

A small octahedron of what may be sphalerite or galena is near the white calcite in this photo.

Rockhounding

Shullsburg was a key mining community in southwest Wisconsin, and is one of the oldest cities in Wisconsin. Its founder, Jesse Shull, came to the area in 1818 and was a fur trader working for John Jacob Astor, the president of American Fur Company. Legend has it that he was walking and stopped for lunch, and saw a badger digging near a spring. When he checked the badger's diggings he found small pieces of metallic ores. Other reports indicate that Native Americans showed him the rich ore deposits in 1826, but the badger story is better. Like all mineral rushes, miners quickly came to the area. Many deposits were near the surface and the miners were called "badgers" as they dug thousands of shallow holes. Wisconsin was subsequently nicknamed the "Badger State."

The community was originally named New Dublin since it was mainly Irish miners until the early 1840s. Lead mining was the main industry and the town prospered, but the Civil War took a toll, despite the production of lead for bullets. The mines were worked during the late nineteenth century and into the twentieth century. In 1934 butter and cheese were produced in

The chert lenses are abundant in this outcrop and can be seen just above the hammer.

Shullsburg, which became the second major industry for the region. Many of the mines produced lead into the 1940s. The last mining operation ceased in 1979 when the Eagle-Picher mine closed. Ironically southwest Wisconsin went from producing lead, which poisoned many through lead paint and leaded gasoline, to cheese, which now contributes to worldwide obesity.

Unfortunately, virtually all the remains of the mines are on private property and cannot be accessed without permission. The USGS topographic map for the region shows mines throughout the area, but many have been completely obliterated by development and reclamation. In a mining district like this, the best way to find minerals is to look at accessible outcrops at roadcuts.

WI 11 has such an outcrop approximately 1.9 miles west of Shullsburg. This is an outcrop of Ordovician limestone and dolostone. Parking is available on the north side of the highway on the shoulder just east of the outcrop.

This is an interesting outcrop, as it is a brown sandy limestone/dolostone with several depressions, some of which have small veins of weathered calcite. On close inspection I found that some of these had small black octahedrons.

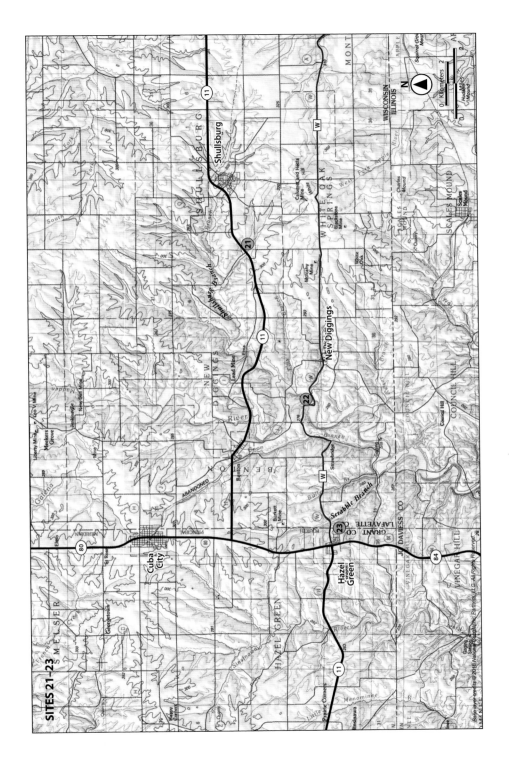

SITES 21-23

I thought these were sphalerite but they may also be galena. I wish I could say these were abundant, but I did not see many of them. I suspect that if I spent more time looking I might have found more.

I was soon distracted by the multiple lenses of orange to light brown chert. While chert lenses are common in the Sinnippee Group sediments in this part of Wisconsin, they are easy to see here as the outcrop is nearly vertical and they stand out in the weathered sediments.

While this roadcut does not have abundant metallic minerals, the white calcite and small metallic mineral octahedrons are an indication that you are within the Shullsburg mining district. The chert itself makes this roadcut worth a stop, but I think you may be able to find more octahedrons with some effort.

References: USGS, 2004. Johnson, 2017

22. New Diggings Calcite

The shoulders are wide and you can park at the roadcut instead of the nearby parking area if needed.

County: Lafayette
Site type: Roadcut
Land status: Highway right-of-way
Material: Ordovician limestone and dolostone
Host rock: Ordovician Sinnippee Group limestone and dolostone
Difficulty: Easy
Family-friendly: Yes
Tools needed: Hammer
Special concerns: Traffic on WI 11
Special attractions: Fishing in the Galena River
GPS parking: N42° 32.467' / W90° 21.183'
GPS calcite in roadcut: N42° 32.517' / W90° 21.383'
Topographic quadrangle: New Diggings, WI-IL
Finding the site: From New Diggings, at the intersection of CR-W and CR-I, take CR-W approximately 1.0 mile to a parking area on the south (left) side of CR-W

The rocks have many veins and vugs filled with calcite.

on the east bank of the Galena River. This is a parking area for access to fish in the Galena River. Park here and walk to the outcrops, which are where CR-W makes a curve to the north. The calcite is found primarily at the location of the GPS coordinates above. Alternatively, the shoulder on CR-W is wide and should be adequate for parking. This would eliminate the need to walk across the bridge over the Galena River, which can be dangerous if there is a lot of traffic.

Rockhounding

New Diggings is not new. It is one of the oldest communities in Wisconsin. It reportedly got its name when miners from Galena, Illinois, which was known as the "Old Diggings" came north to work the lead mines of southwest Wisconsin. The lead mines were first developed in the 1820s. Many of the workers were experienced Cornish miners, and lead production peaked in the 1840s. During the California Gold Rush of 1849 many of the best miners abandoned the lead mines for the gold fields. The Civil War came shortly afterward and lead production never recovered to its prior peaks. In 1860 the deposits began to be worked for zinc as well as lead. The district continued producing zinc and lead throughout World War II, but virtually all the zinc

Fist-sized masses of crystalline calcite can be found in parts of this roadcut, especially on the north side.

and lead mines in southwest Wisconsin closed shortly after the war. The mines could not compete with larger deposits, and the demand for both lead and zinc could no longer sustain the local industry.

I first visited this site in 2003 when exploring the region for collecting sites. I knew the area had several mines, and I thought that a place called New Diggings was a good place to start. I could not find any accessible mines, but I found some excellent calcite at this roadcut just west of the Galena River. Fortunately I had my GPS and was able to record the location. This paid off when I visited the area in May 2017, as I had recorded the coordinates in my field book and still had them accessible nearly 14 years after my visit.

The calcite is easiest to find by using the GPS coordinates above. Most of the calcite is in the roadcut on the north side of CR-W near the western end of the roadcut. You can find loose calcite in pieces below the rocks of the roadcut, but you can also find it in small veins. Freshly broken calcite shows excellent cleavage at this site, and many of the veins have aggregates of small white calcite crystals. I did not see any large metallic minerals, but I noticed that many of the vein calcite pieces that I found were extremely dense and appeared to have finely disseminated oxides and sulfides. Further exploration of this roadcut may also show that it has some galena and sphalerite as well as the calcite.

References: USGS, 2004; Johnson, 2017

23. Hazel Green Pyrite and Sphalerite

County: Grant
Site type: Rocks in drainage ditch
Land status: Uncertain, not posted
Material: Mining waste rocks
Host rock: Mineralized Ordovician Sinnippee Group limestone and dolostone
Difficulty: Easy
Family-friendly: Yes
Tools needed: Hammer
Special concerns: Tricky footing in ditch, easy to trip and fall
Special attractions: Hardscrabble Prairie State Natural Area
GPS parking: N42° 31.733' / W90° 25.650'
Topographic quadrangle: Cuba City, WI-IL
Finding the site: This site is at the eastern end of 14th St in Hazel Green. From WI 80 in Hazel Green, go east on 16th St for about 0.2 mile. It ends at Birch Street. Turn right (south) on Birch Street, and proceed about 0.1 mile to 14th St. Proceed about 0.2 mile to the end of 14th St, and park on the right side of the road. The rocks are in a wide drainage ditch along the south side of 14th St.

Rockhounding

Hazel Green is near the southwestern corner of the lead–zinc mining region of southwestern Wisconsin. The town was originally named "Hardscrabble," after a fight over a lead mine between James Hardy and Moses Meeker. Hardy was the winner, and the fight was referred to as the Hardy Scrape, which later morphed into Hardscrabble. This was not an attractive name for the town, so the town later took the name Hazel Green after the hazel bushes in the area.

The mines around Hazel Green closed entirely by the mid-twentieth century, and many of the mines closed long before then. Virtually all the former mine sites are on private land so it is difficult to get access to collecting sites. In these cases, I have found that the best option is to use Google Maps and Google Earth to check satellite imagery for accessible areas, and most importantly, indications of rocks. Often if you can find a roadcut or rock pile there is a good possibility of finding minerals related to the mines.

The drainage ditch is full of waste rock from local mines.

This rock is almost solid pyrite, and it was broken off a rock from the drainage ditch.

The sulfide minerals on the rocks are easy to spot as they are often intergrown with calcite and limonite.

When reviewing the satellite imagery for Hazel Green I came across what appeared to be a large ditch full of rocks along the south side of 14th St. I recorded the coordinates and went to this site when I visited Hazel Green.

The north side of 14th St appeared to be the local sewer plant. A composting facility, which is open to the public, is next to the plant. I parked at the end of 14th St and walked to the drainage ditch. It was overgrown with vegetation, but it was full of large rocks. Just as I suspected, the rocks were waste rocks from a former mine. Nearly all of the rocks were mineralized and the minerals included pyrite, chalcopyrite, sphalerite, malachite, and galena. The rocks were rounded and extremely hard, and it was hard to break any pieces off the rocks. However, one of the first boulders I hammered was a highly mineralized rock. I knocked a fragment off that was nearly solid gold pyrite. The pyrite radiated from different points in the rock. The rock also had some chalcopyrite.

I later walked further up the drainage. I found many more mineralized rocks, and most of what I found was goethite, pyrite, chalcopyrite, sphalerite, malachite, and minor galena. The rocks continued as far as I could see. According to the satellite imagery the rocks extend along the entire length of south 14th St, so there are plenty more rocks to check out. This is an excellent site to see some of the rocks that were produced from the local mines, even though the mining company likely considered the rocks as waste.

References: Chicago and Northwestern Railway Company, 1908; USGS, 2004; Johnson, 2017; Saggio, 2017

24. Platteville Fossils

County: Grant
Site type: Roadcut
Land status: Uncertain, not posted
Material: Fossils in Limestone
Host rock: Ordovician Galena Dolomite and Decorah Formation
Difficulty: Easy
Family-friendly: No, too much traffic
Tools needed: Hammer
Special concerns: Traffic on US 151
Special attractions: Mining and Rollo Jamison Museums in Platteville
GPS parking-Galena Dolomite: N42º 40.350' / W90º 32.917'
GPS parking-Decorah Shale/Limestone: N42º 40.167' / W90º 33.033'
Topographic quadrangle: Dickeyville, WI
Finding the site: From the intersection of CR-D and US 151, proceed west and then southwest for 4.8 miles. You will approach a large roadcut on the right (west) side of US 151. Park on the shoulder at a safe place. This is the Galena Dolomite roadcut. From here, you can either drive or park to the next roadcut on US 151, which is Decorah Shale and Limestone.

Rockhounding

As you travel southwest from Platteville, US 151 descends into the valley of the Little Platte River and exposes a thick section of Ordovician dolomite, limestone, shale, and sandstone. From youngest to oldest you start in the Galena Dolomite and drive pass cliffs of Decorah Formation, Platteville Formation, St. Peter Sandstone, and end at the Prairie Du Chien Dolomite as you enter the Little Platte River valley.

The first outcrop for this locality exposes the Galena Dolomite. This is a light brown, sandy, vuggy dolomite. This is an interesting roadcut but fossils were not common at the exposure that I reviewed. However, I may have been looking in a part of the section that did not have many fossils. The lower part of the Galena Dolomite reportedly has more limestone and sections are reported to have fossils, so it may be worth exploring this roadcut in more detail. It is a long roadcut with many more areas to explore.

The second outcrop exposes the Decorah Formation, which at this roadcut consists of limestone and dolomite. This outcrop is a distinct gray and

Slabs of fossils can be found in the loose rocks at the base of the roadcut.

does not have the vuggy character of the dolomite at the previous roadcut. The limestone at this cut has many fossils. The best way to find the fossils is to look at the loose pieces of limestone at the base of the roadcut. Most of them are small brachiopods and they are easy to see on the weathered limestone surfaces. A hammer is only needed to trim the pieces, as you will not find more fossils by breaking the rocks apart.

When I parked at this site I stayed as far off the road as possible. I was later sitting in the driver's seat of my car confirming my GPS coordinates in my field book when I heard a tap on the passenger side window. A highway patrol car, with his lights flashing, had parked behind me, and the policeman was at my side window. I was so engrossed in my notes that I did not even notice that he had pulled up behind me.

I got out of the car and explained that I was a geologist looking for fossils in the roadcut. I had my orange safety vest and hard hat and emphasized that I was well off the road and careful along the sides of the roadcut. He was completely fine with this and said that it was just their policy to check anyone who was stopped on the roadside to see if they needed help. I was extremely

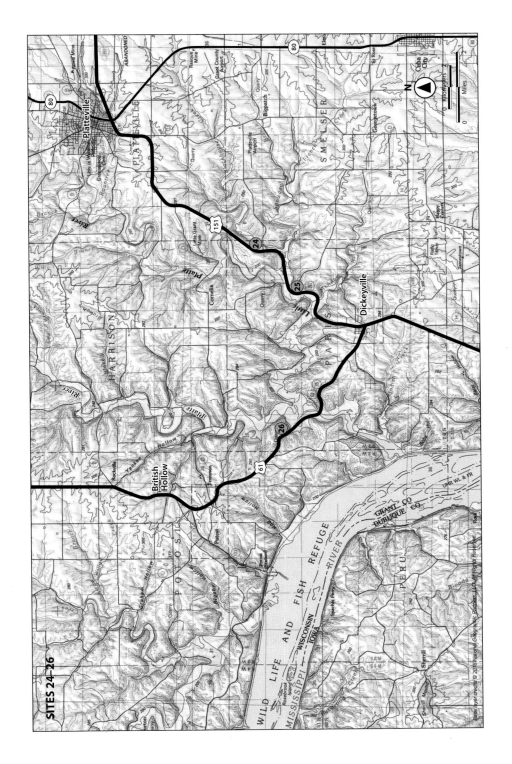

SITES 24–26

glad that I did not get a ticket for unauthorized stopping. Since this is a US route, and not an interstate, stopping on the side of the road, as long as you are well outside of traffic, is not a problem, but we always like to minimize interaction with law enforcement as they have many more serious issues to deal with on our roads. If you stop at this site, keep in mind that there is a high likelihood that you will also be stopped by the highway patrol to make sure that you have not broken down or have any other problems. Most of the time I do not have any issues with the police but it is always important to be prepared if you do.

As you continue southwest on US 151 toward Dickeyville, additional exposures of Decorah, Platteville, St. Peter Sandstone, and Prairie du Chien formations are further exposed in roadcuts. If you can find a safe place to pull over these may all be worth checking out. The only one of these formations that does not have fossils is the St. Peter Sandstone, but this may have some interesting sections of sandstone so it should not be ruled out as a potential stop.

References: Agnew et al., 1956; Whitlow and West, 1966

25. Dickeyville Ordovician White Sandstone

County: Grant
Site type: Roadcut
Land status: Uncertain, not posted
Material: White and orange sandstone with banding
Host rock: Ordovician St. Peter Sandstone
Difficulty: Easy
Family-friendly: Yes
Tools needed: Hammer
Special concerns: Must park as far as possible off road
Special attractions: Mining and Rollo Jamison Museums in Platteville
GPS parking: N42° 39.350' / W90° 34.400'
Topographic quadrangle: Dickeyville, WI
Finding the site: From Dickeyville at exit 8, take US 151 northeast for 2.8 miles to the intersection with Clay Hollow Road. This will be on the right (east) side of the highway. You will see a large exposure of white sandstone in the cliffs just before Clay Hollow Road. Park on the shoulder and walk to the outcrop.

Rockhounding

US 151 in southwest Wisconsin has many excellent exposures of sandstone and limestone, but this exposure stands out due to the color and bedding. The sandstone is generally white and orange and has some attractive banded areas. I noticed this exposure when driving to Platteville and immediately stopped when I saw that I could safely pull over onto the shoulder near Clay Hollow Road. This is an excellent location to see the St. Peter Sandstone firsthand and at a site that is not actively mined.

The St. Peter Sandstone was named after the St. Peter River in Minnesota. The sandstone is found in several Midwestern states, including Minnesota, Illinois, Indiana, Missouri, Iowa, and Wisconsin. It is generally considered to be a marine sand deposited near the shore of an advancing sea. The sandstone is nearly all quartz and the grains are well sorted and rounded.

The high purity, rounded grains, and consistent character made the St. Peter Sandstone an important formation for many industrial purposes.

Limonite and hematite bands can also be seen in pieces of the sandstone.

These include glass sand, ceramics, paint additive, molding sand, and filters. One of the most important recent uses for the St. Peter Sandstone has been as hydraulic fracturing sand for the oil and gas industry, and it is often known as "frack sand."

At this locality the formation is overlain by the Platteville Formation and then the Decorah Formation, both of which are limestone, dolostone, and shale. The top of the ridge is Galena Dolomite. The exposure is well away from the road so traffic is not a problem. The sandstone is white to orange. It is poorly cemented and crumbles easily when hit with a hammer. However, you can use the pick end of your hammer to extract large pieces. They will crumble under pressure but remain largely intact if you are careful.

It is interesting to observe this sandstone under a hand lens or microscope to see the purity of the quartz and the uniform size of the rounded grains. They were washed, reworked, and sorted over millions of years. You cannot easily reproduce this type of sand in modern sand deposits, despite lots of

The sandstone has some orange sections as well as bright white.

screening and sorting. Deposits of St. Peter Sandstone, if they are in an area that can be mined and are near a local market, are an important industrial resource.

References: Dapples, 1955; Owen, 1852; Whitlow and West, 1966

26. Dickeyville Ordovician Fossils

County: Grant
Site type: Roadcut
Land status: Uncertain, not posted
Material: Fossils in Limestone
Host rock: Ordovician Platteville Formation
Difficulty: Easy
Family-friendly: Yes
Tools needed: Hammer
Special concerns: Limited parking on highway
Special attractions: Nelson Dewey State Park
GPS parking: N42º 39.567' / W90º 39.167'
Topographic quadrangle: Potosi, WI
Finding the site: From the intersection of Great River Road and US 61/WI 35, take US 61/WI 35 4.1 miles northwest. You will see a long roadcut in the limestone. Park at the location of the coordinates. You can then walk along the roadcut, which is protected from the highway by a guardrail.

Rockhounding

This is an accessible long roadcut that has fossils in limestone. The host rock is the Platteville Formation, which overlies the St. Peter Sandstone. The Platteville Formation consists of four different members. From oldest to youngest, these are the Glenwood Shale, Pecatonica Dolomite, McGregor Limestone, and Quimby's Mill limestone and shale. The Platteville Formation is only about 49 to 55 feet thick in southwest Wisconsin, but since it is nearly horizontal, it is exposed over a wide area.

The rock at this roadcut appears to be mainly limestone, but it may also have some dolomite. I am uncertain which member this represents, but it is certainly almost all carbonate rock. The fossils are not numerous but they are still fairly easy to find. I found several brachiopods and ostracods. Bryozoans and crinoids are also reported to occur at this roadcut, but I did not see any of them.

Small Brachiopods and ostracods are the most common fossils at this locality.

Like most limestone/dolostone fossil localities, it is best to find large pieces of broken rocks and look for fossils on the weathered surfaces. This is a relatively safe place to collect since you are protected by a guard rail, but parking is limited to small cars.

References: Nehm and Bemis, 2002; Whitlow and West, 1966

27. Fennimore Ordovician Fossils

County: Grant
Site type: Roadcut
Land status: Uncertain, not posted
Material: Fossils in Limestone
Host rock: Ordovician Ancell Group Limestone
Difficulty: Easy
Family-friendly: Yes
Tools needed: Hammer
Special concerns: Limited parking on highway
Special attractions: None
GPS parking: N42° 54.467' / W90° 39.983'
Topographic quadrangle: Fennimore, WI
Finding the site: From the intersection of US 18 and US 61 in Fennimore, take US 61 6.1 miles south. Look for a small driveway entrance on the left (east) side of the highway, and park here. The main roadcut is just north of the parking area and on the east side of the road, and a smaller roadcut is on the west side of the road.

Rockhounding

This is a fairly long roadcut that exposes limestone of the Ordovician Ancell Group. Fossils are common in this roadcut. Fossils reported in the roadcuts south of Fennimore include brachiopods, trilobites, ostracods, bryozoans, and cephalopods.

Parking here is limited to about one car, but fortunately it is at an unpaved driveway entrance. It is best to position your car well to the site and facing the highway so you do not block anyone that may need to use the driveway. The roadcut can then be accessed by a short walk from your car. There is a small grassy swale between US 61 and the roadcut, so it is very easy to walk along the roadcut and stay well away from traffic. However, it is still a good idea to have a high-visibility vest when at any roadcut.

The rocks at this site are mainly a brownish-gray limestone with some sandy sections. The best fossils are found in the loose gray limestone pieces at the base of the roadcut. A hammer is useful for trimming pieces, but nearly all the fossils that you will find are on weathered surfaces. I found several pieces with brachiopods and some ostracods, but did not find any pieces with

Aggregates of fossils are common in the loose rocks at the base of the roadcut.

bryozoans, trilobites, or cephalopods. Most of the pieces with fossils were flat pieces of limestone with an assemblage of small brachiopods. I checked the roadcuts on the west side of the road, but did not find any significant differences from the east side. I preferred the east side as it exposes more rocks and was better exposed in the late afternoon soon.

References: Nehm and Bemis, 2002; USGS, 2004

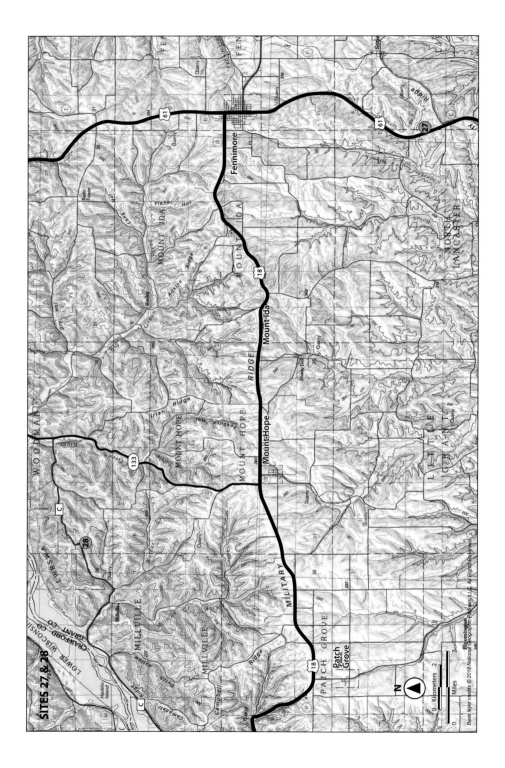

SITES 27 & 28

28. Millville Ordovician Fossils

County: Grant
Site type: Former roadside quarry
Land status: Uncertain, not posted
Material: Fossils in Dolostone
Host rock: Ordovician Prairie du Chien Group Dolostone
Difficulty: Easy
Family-friendly: Yes
Tools needed: Hammer
Special concerns: Land status uncertain
Special attractions: Adiantum Woods State Natural Area
GPS parking: N43° 02.683' / W90° 53.933'
Topographic quadrangle: Wauzeka West, WI
Finding the site: Start at the intersection of CR-C and Millville Hollow Road in Millville. Proceed east on CR-C for 2.1 miles. On the left (north) side of CR-C you will see a small roadcut that was likely a small roadside quarry. Park here and make sure you are well off the road.

Rockhounding

The rocks exposed at this site are dolostones of the Lower Ordovician Prairie du Chien Group. The Prairie du Chien Group is primarily dolostone with some sandstone and shale. From oldest to youngest, it consists of the Oneota Dolomite, the New Richmond Sandstone, and the Shakopee Dolomite. The Prairie du Chien Group is approximately 300 feet thick, and is extensively exposed throughout southwestern Wisconsin. It is named for the type locality near Prairie du Chien in Crawford County, Wisconsin. The Prairie du Chien was deposited in shallow, warm seas located in near the equator during the Lower Ordovician. The thickest unit, which is the Oneota dolomite, forms high cliffs along the major stream valleys.

At this location, I am not sure which part of the Prairie du Chien group is exposed. This is a small roadside locality that I stopped at near twilight in May 2017. It resembled a small roadside quarry and it was not posted, and I was able to park at the location. The rock at this location is a light gray carbonate. The bedding of the rocks is nearly horizontal. Several large blocks of carbonate had broken off the highwalls, which were only about 20 feet high. Much of the carbonate near the top of the highwalls was thinly bedded.

The surfaces of many of the large rocks in the quarry are covered with fossils.

Fossils are common in the carbonate blocks of the base of the quarry. Most of what I found were brachiopods, and many of them were in fragments and exposed on weathered surfaces of the carbonate. This is a good locality to check out if you would like to grab large pieces with abundant Lower Ordovician fossils.

References: Burgess, 2013; Heyl et al., 1951; USGS, 2004

29. Plum Creek Chert

The chert is best exposed by breaking apart rocks that appear to have interiors of chert.

County: Crawford
Site type: Creekbed
Land status: Fishing Access area
Material: Chert
Host rock: Gravels derived from Ordovician and Cambrian Dolostones
Difficulty: Easy
Family-friendly: Yes
Tools needed: Hammer
Special concerns: Dry creek may become flooded
Special attractions: Fishing on Plum Creek
GPS parking: N43° 08.017' / W90° 56.117'
Topographic quadrangle: Crowley Ridge, WI
Finding the site: From WI 60 in Wauzeka, turn left (north) on CR-N. Continue on CR for 0.8 mile, and then take the right fork to Plum Creek Road. Continue on

Plum Creek Road for 3.3 miles. Continue on Plum Creek Road by turning a sharp left (west) as you approach Shanghai Ridge Road. Continue 1.3 miles on Plum Creek Road, and the parking area is to the left (south). It is marked as a fishing access for Plum Creek, and parking is available for one or two cars at the most. From here you can walk either east or west in the small drainage next to the parking area.

Rockhounding

Although this site is next to Plum Creek, it is important to emphasize that the locality is not in Plum Creek. Plum Creek is a good-sized trout stream, and while it undoubtedly has some chert within its banks, it is not really accessible unless you want to spend time in a cold water stream. The locality is actually a dry tributary that is adjacent to the parking area. Interestingly, I am not sure when this would get water. At this time of my visit in late May 2017 many of the local rivers were at flood stage, but this small tributary was dry. This suggests that while it may become flooded during local events, it may remain dry even when other rivers are flooding.

Chert is abundant in this dry creek bed. The chert weathers out of Cambrian and Ordovician dolomites, and it can be found loose in the dry creek bed. Some of the chert resembles translucent agate, and sometimes it is difficult to tell the difference between agate and chert, as both are cryptocrystalline silica. Some of the pieces are opaque and resemble chunks of porcelain. You will want to have a hammer to trim pieces and to break apart larger pieces. The chert is generally light gray to light brown, and is easy to spot in the former creek bed.

Reference: USGS, 2004

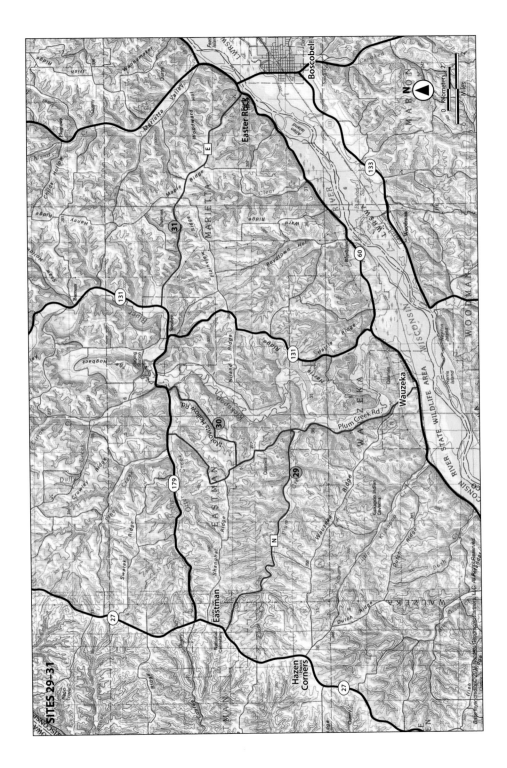

SITES 29–31

30. Walker Hollow Road Chert

Some of the chert is banded and can be found loose on the ground.

County: Crawford
Site type: Rocks adjacent to quarry
Land status: Not posted, uncertain
Material: Chert
Host rock: Ordovician Prairie du Chien Group Dolostone
Difficulty: Easy
Family-friendly: Yes, but best when nearby quarry is not operating
Tools needed: Hammer
Special concerns: Stay away when quarry active due to traffic
Special attractions: None
GPS parking: N43° 09.833' / W90° 54.500'
Topographic quadrangle: Crowley Ridge, WI
Finding the site: From the intersection of WI 179, which is also Ferris Street, and WI 131 in Steuben, go west on Ferris Street for 1.9 miles. Turn left (south) on Walker Hollow Road. Proceed 1.8 miles, and you will see a large quarry on the

Loose rocks and outcrops are present across the road from the quarry.

south side of Walker Hollow Road. Park on the shoulder of the road outside of the quarry. The chert can be found as loose rock on the ground and in boulders on the sides of the road.

Rockhounding

This is an active quarry that is on the south side of Walker Hollow Road. These quarries are common in the Prairie du Chien dolostone in southwest Wisconsin. At the time of my visit on a Friday morning in May 2017, the quarry was not operating. It likely only operates when the quarry operator gets an order for stone.

You can park on the roadside away from the quarry and look at the rocks in outcrop and loose pieces on the ground. The rocks outside the quarry and the roadside are primarily dolostones, and some of them have pieces of chert in the matrix of the rock. The chert is primarily white and gray, and many of the pieces are banded. Most pieces are small but many are softball sized. A hammer is useful for trimming and breaking apart the chert to expose unweathered sections. The best chert seems to be the loose larger pieces that are found on the ground, and they are often obscured by grass and dirt.

Reference: USGS, 2004

31. Boscobel Dolostone-Sandstone Quarry

County: Crawford
Site type: Roadside quarry
Land status: Not posted, uncertain
Material: Chert
Host rock: Cambrian/Ordovician Dolostone and Sandstone
Difficulty: Easy
Family-friendly: Yes
Tools needed: Hammer
Special concerns: Land Status Uncertain, must stay away from highwalls
Special attractions: Blue River Bluffs State Natural Area
GPS parking: N43º 10.583' / W90º 47.683'
Topographic quadrangle: Steuben, WI
Finding the site: From the intersection of WI 60 and CR-E, just northwest of Boscobel, proceed west for 4.5 miles on CR-E. The quarry will be on the right (north) side of the road. Park here and walk directly to the quarry.

Rockhounding

This is an inactive quarry that is on the north side of CR-E. These quarries are common in the region. They are worth checking out if you can find a safe place to park and observe the quarry if it is not posted against trespassing.

This quarry is mapped as within Cambrian dolostone and sandstone. The beds are nearly horizontal, and the rocks near the top of the highwall appear to be dolostone as they are gray and exhibit some dissolution cavities that are common in dolostone in southwest Wisconsin. The rocks in the section near the base of the quarry are primarily sandstones. Based on the exposures in the quarry the rocks may be Cambrian sandstones at the base of the highwalls and Ordovician Prairie du Chien Dolostone overlying the Cambrian sediments. The rocks found at the base of the highwall, of course, also include the rocks that have fallen from the top of the quarry, so the rocks at the bottom are a mix of dolostone and sandstone. These rocks have abundant gray and black chert, and the minerals include pyrite, cubes of limonite after pyrite, and iron-stained quartz.

Reference: USGS, 2004

A limonite after pyrite cube is on the right side of this rock.

There are abundant rock piles near the highwalls and you must be careful of falling rocks.

32. Reads Creek Chert

The chert can be found in the loose rocks in Reads Creek.

County: Vernon
Site type: Stream bed
Land status: Uncertain, not posted
Material: Brown, yellow, and white chert
Host rock: Gravels derived from Ordovician and Cambrian Dolostones
Difficulty: Easy
Family-friendly: Yes
Tools needed: Hammer
Special concerns: Mosquitoes, land status along creek
Special attractions: Fishing in Reads Creek
GPS parking: N43° 28.733' / W90° 49.717'
GPS stream bed: N43° 28.617' / W90° 49.767'
Topographic quadrangle: Readstown, WI

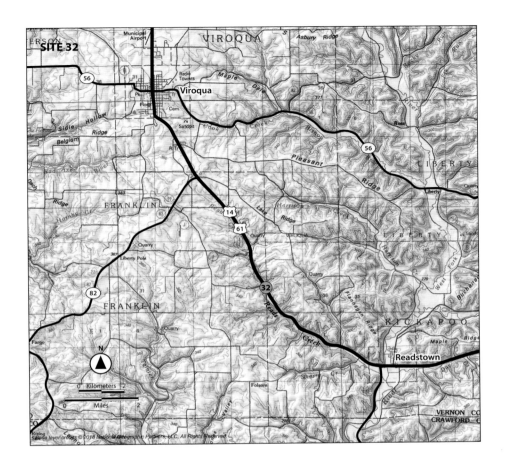

Finding the site: From the intersection of US 61 and US 14 in Readstown, take US 61 northwest for 4.0 miles. You will reach a small wayside park on the right (east) side of US 61. Park here, and walk across US 61 to CR-JJ, and walk to Reads Creek. At this time this was written, the bridge across Reads Creek was closed to traffic due to flood damage. Climb down the embankment, and the chert can be found in the creek bed rocks.

Rockhounding

I originally visited this site to look for copper mineralization, which was reported to occur on both sides of Reads Creek. Unfortunately the area is heavily wooded, and I did not see any outcrops exposed on the area hillsides. However, I walked into Reads Creek from CR-JJ. The bridge had been damaged and it was possible to walk across it, but it was closed to traffic.

The chert ranges from light brown to white.

Reads Creek was fairly low and I was able to see a lot of the rocks in the creek. Most of them were dolostones with some Precambrian glacial rocks including gneissic and granitic rocks. I did not see any indications of copper minerals. However, I took a second look at what else might be in the creek, and I noticed some large pieces of white chert. Breaking these open revealed that some of the chert was brown and yellow. The chert is most abundant on some of the small islands and rocky bars. Although I did not see any copper minerals, it may be worth it to the surrounding area for indications of copper, but the chert alone makes this a good site for rockhounds.

References: Cordua, 1998; Heyl and West, 1982; USGS, 2004

33. Ableman's Gorge Quartz Crystals

The core of the former quarry is nearly vertical Proterozoic quartzite.

County: Sauk
Site type: Former quarry
Land status: State Natural Area
Material: Quartz crystals
Host rock: Precambrian Baraboo Quartzite
Difficulty: Easy
Family-friendly: Yes
Tools needed: None, collecting not allowed
Special concerns: No collecting allowed
Special attractions: Devils Lake State Park
GPS parking: N43° 29.000' / W89° 55.050'
GPS quartz crystals: N43° 29.133' / W89° 55.100'

Veins of small clear to translucent quartz crystals are abundant near the northeastern end of the former quarry.

Topographic quadrangle: Rock Springs, WI
Finding the site: Start at the intersection of West Broadway Street and River Road in Rock Springs. Take River Road, which is also known as WI 136, north for 0.6 mile. You will be able to see the large abandoned quarry on the west side of road. Park on the west side of the road just north of the turnout for a water spring. From here you can walk to the former quarry.

Rockhounding

This site is just north of Rock Springs and is located in the Upper Narrows of the Baraboo River. The area is known as Ableman's Gorge, and it is a classic locality for geologists. The site was designated a State Natural Area in 1969. The west side of the road has a long abandoned quarry that is now owned by the Wisconsin Department of Natural Resources and the University of Wisconsin. The quarry produced aggregate from the Baraboo Quartzite, which is a reddish-brown Precambrian quartzite. The beds of the quartzite are nearly vertical, and the quartzite was eroded into a Precambrian "island." Cambrian

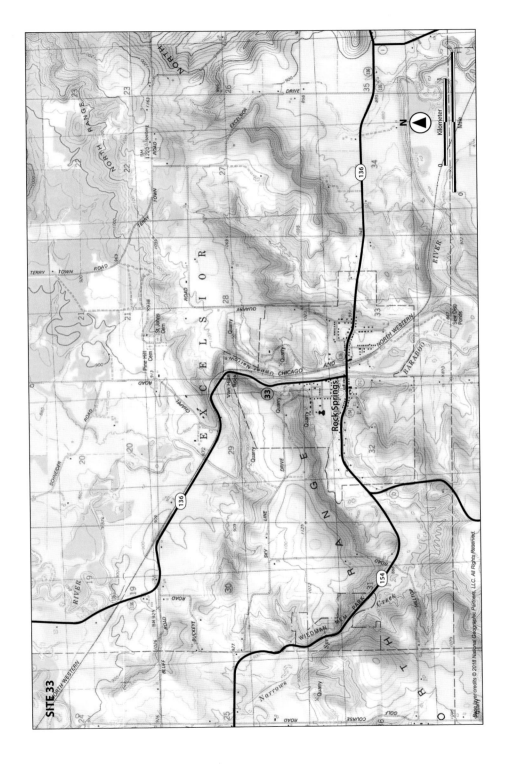

SITE 33

sandstones were then deposited on top of the quartzite unconformably along the sides of the quartzite. It is hard to comprehend the amount of time that it took from the initial deposition of the Precambrian sands to their metamorphism to quartzite, tilting to vertical, erosion, and then deposition of Cambrian sediments, which are very old themselves.

I first visited the area in 2005 during a trip through central Wisconsin. I parked near a spring east of WI 136 and walked to a large abandoned quarry. I also visited the area in May 2017 and found that much of the quarry remained the same. A hiking trail is still along the quarry floor, and it is easy to walk in the quarry. The Baraboo Quartzite shows excellent cross-bedding and has various shades of brownish red and gray. Quartz crystals can be seen along veinlets in the quartzite, and some aggregates of crystals can be found on the ground. I found that the quartz crystals were most abundant in the northeastern end of the former quarry. It is possible to climb onto some of the rock piles near the highwalls, but as always you must be careful of falling rocks. I saw some people who climbed around the back of the quarry and later were perched on the highwalls. The highwalls are nearly 200 feet high and I do not recommend spending time on the edges of the highwalls.

If you go to this site, be sure to stop by the Van Hise Rock, which is just north of the gorge and on the east side of the road. The rock, named for Charles Van Hise, shows some of structures that are found within the quarry. Van Hise developed many of his principles of structural deformation and metamorphism through studying the rocks of this area.

References: Daziel and Dott, 1970; Dott and Attig, 2004

34. Arcadia Sandstone Concretions

The roadcut offers excellent views of the Cambrian stratigraphic section in the region.

County: Trempealeau
Site type: Roadcut
Land status: Uncertain, not posted
Material: White sandstone concretions
Host rock: Cambrian Jordan Formation sandstone
Difficulty: Easy
Family-friendly: Yes
Tools needed: Hammer
Special concerns: Traffic
Special attractions: None
GPS parking: N44° 11.817' / W91° 27.650'
GPS outcrops: N44° 11.867' / W91° 27.633'

Some of the concretions occur in large well-cemented sandstones.

Topographic quadrangle: Tamarack, WI
Finding the site: From the intersection of WI 95 and WI 93 in Arcadia, proceed south on WI 93 for 3.9 miles. You will see some large exposures of sandstone on both sides of the road. Turn right (west) on Addelman Lane, and park off this unpaved road on the shoulder. You can then walk to the outcrops from here.

Rockhounding

I learned about this site through a 2012 field guidebook on a conference on Silica Sand Resources of Minnesota and Wisconsin. Conference guidebooks are often an excellent resource for finding rockhounding sites. This guidebook included a field stop at a silica sand roadcut south of Arcadia in Trempealeau County. What caught my attention was a picture of hundreds of round calcareous nodules on the sandstone surface. I had seen these on top of the St. Peter Sandstone in Missouri, but I had not found an accessible outcrop with them in several years.

The outcrop was described as in the Cambrian Jordan Formation, and the Ordovician Oneota Formation is exposed in cliffs above the Jordan

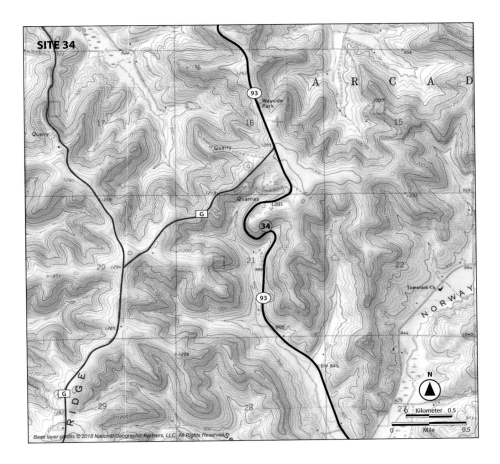

Formation. The Jordan Formation has coarse-grained, well-rounded quartz grains and it is highly prized as a resource for hydraulic fracturing sand for the oil and gas industry.

The roadcuts south of Arcadia are known for providing nearly complete exposures of Cambrian stratigraphy. At this roadcut, the Van Oser member of the Jordan Formation is exposed at road level. This member has the highly desired medium–coarse-grained sandstone, and it disaggregates easily. It is the main member of the Jordan Formation that is extracted for hydraulic fracturing sand at nearby mines. These mines are easily visible on the satellite photographs of the area.

We stopped at this outcrop in September 2017. I surveyed on the western side of the roadcut for the calcareous nodules but could not find any. I was

The concretions often occur in rounded masses like grapes, but these are fragile and easily broken.

initially frustrated, but we soon found some small nodules and this offered encouragement. We then went to the eastern side of the highway near the southern end of the exposures. We soon found an incredible amount of nodules.

The nodules generally ranged in size from a pea to a large marble. The most interesting pieces we found were large aggregates of round nodules. These were fragile and they would break easily if they came in contact with other rocks. We also found some large slabs of sandstone with nodules on their surface. This is definitely one of the most interesting exposures of Cambrian sandstone that we have visited in Wisconsin. The location map does not show current configuration of WI 93. It should also be noted that WI 93 has been straightened and does not have the curves shown in the location map for this site.

References: Syverson et al., 2012; Ostrom, 1987; Runkel, 1994, Runkel, 2000

35. Hanley Road Vuggy Dolostone

County: St. Croix
Site type: Roadcut
Land status: Not posted, adjacent to roadway
Material: Quartz and carbonate crystals in vugs
Host rock: Ordovician Prairie du Chien Dolostone
Difficulty: Easy
Family-friendly: Yes
Tools needed: Hammer
Special concerns: Land status uncertain
Special attractions: Willow River State Park
GPS parking: N44° 57.283' / W92° 43.183'
GPS roadcut: N44° 57.250' / W92° 42.933'
Topographic quadrangle: Northline, WI-MN
Finding the site: From I-94, take exit 2 to Carmichael Road and head south.
Go approximately 0.9 mile, and turn left (east) onto Hanley Road. Proceed about
0.3 mile, and you will be in the middle of the large roadcut. I suggest parking at
one of the parking lots for commercial businesses just west Pearson Drive, which
is west of the roadcut. One of these businesses is a coffee shop, and I recommend
parking as a customer for a cup of coffee or other transaction so you can park as
a customer before a short walk to the roadcut. You can also park Weitkamp Park,
which is north of Hanley Road, but you have to walk a much longer way to get to
the roadcut.

Rockhounding

This is a relatively recent roadcut exposed when Hanley Road was built to
serve the industrial park and surrounding area. It exposes nearly horizontal
beds of the Ordovician Oneota Formation Dolostone of the Prairie du Chien
Group. It does not show up on the USGS topographic map for the region, but
the version that I use is quite old (1974), so this is not surprising.

This is one of the best and most accessible exposures of the Oneota
Formation in the Prairie du Chien Group that I have seen in western
Wisconsin. Hanley Road is extremely busy, but there is actually an asphalt–
paved walking path along the south side of the road.

Fortunately the area is not posted, but there are warning signs against
climbing on the cliffs. This is an important field trip stop for geologists in the

The vugs are filled with quartz or calcite and can be seen in both outcrop or loose rocks.

region, so it tends to get a lot of geologic visitors. The rocks at this area are mainly vuggy dolostones that have quartz, calcite, and aragonite crystals. I did not find any significant fossils.

You should wear a hard hat at this site as the highwalls are sheer and have the potential for falling rocks. A better idea is to stay far away from the highwalls and focus on the loose rocks at the base of the roadcut. Vugs with quartz and calcite crystals are common, but you should allow enough time to find the best specimens. Many of the pieces are solid and do not have crystals, but with a little effort you can find some pieces of vuggy dolostone with crystals. A hammer is useful to trim the pieces and break open suspected voids.

Reference: LePain, 2006

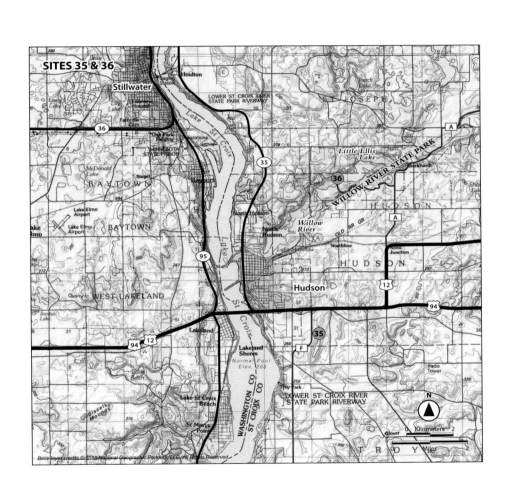

36. Little Falls Dam Cambrian Fossils

Little Falls dam has been removed and the lake is gone, at least for now.

County: St. Croix
Site type: Stream bank
Land status: State Park
Material: Small marine fossils
Host rock: Cambrian Jordan Formation sandstone
Difficulty: Easy
Family-friendly: Yes
Tools needed: None, collecting not allowed
Special concerns: State Park
Special attractions: Willow Falls
GPS parking: N45° 00.917' / W92° 42.333'
GPS dam site fossils: N45° 00.983' / W92° 42.383'

The fossils are very small and some of the rocks resemble coquina.

Topographic quadrangle: Somerset South, WI-MN
Finding the site: From I-94, take exit 4 to US 12, and head north for 1.6 miles, and then US 12 turns into CR-U. Go 0.3 mile north on CR-U, and stay to the right to continue on CR-A. Continue 1.5 miles, and then turn left onto the road to Willow River State Park. You will have to pay an entrance fee to go into the park. Continue on the park access road for about 2 miles, and you will come to a parking area. This is just on the south side of the Little Falls Lake and immediately south of the dam across Willow Creek.

Rockhounding

This is an interesting locality but it must be emphasized that this is a State Park, and as such fossil collecting is not allowed. However, it is still possible to see the fossils in outcrop. The fossils occur in the Cambrian-age Jordan Formation, which is part of the Trempealeau Group in western Wisconsin. The Jordan Formation is a brown-yellow to white sandstone, which ranges from friable to well-cemented fine to coarse-grained quartzose sandstone and siltstone.

At the time of my visit in late May 2017, the Little Falls Lake had been drained for maintenance. The dam had been partially removed and Willow Creek roared through the former south side of the dam. The area was crowded with families, many of whom were fishing.

I had heard that the dam site had fossils, but I did not see any at the dam or in any of the rocks exposed in the dry lake bed. I finally found a fossiliferous outcrop of sandstone just west of the partially removed dam on the south side of Willow Creek. The fossils were very small and consisted of tiny brachiopods and fragment of shells. The fossils are small but abundant. I searched the woods for additional outcrops and loose pieces with fossils, but the best fossils were in the small exposures on the south side of Willow Creek near the dam. These exposures are of horizontal beds and the sandstone is quite friable and is partially fractured in many places.

This is a very scenic place to visit and observe fossils in outcrop. If you have the opportunity it is worthwhile to drive further north to the trailhead for Willow Falls. This trail slopes downward into the canyon and it is about 0.75 mile to walk to Willow Falls, but it's worth the trip. Willow Falls flows over a section of the Prairie du Chien dolostone, and it is interesting to see how the topography has vastly changed by the presence of this dolostone, which generally forms cliffs along creeks and rivers.

Reference: LePain, 2006

CENTRAL PLAIN

37. Redgranite Granite Quarry

The granite is a remarkably uniform fine-grained pinkish-gray granite.

County: Waushara
Site type: Former Quarry
Land status: Village Park
Material: Granite
Host rock: Precambrian granite
Difficulty: Easy
Family-friendly: Yes
Tools needed: None, collecting likely not allowed
Special concerns: Deep water, recommend staying out of lake
Special attractions: Fishing in Redgranite Lake
GPS parking: N44° 02.583' / W89° 05.817'
Topographic quadrangle: Redgranite, WI
Finding the site: From I-41 in Oshkosh, take exit 119 to WI 21. Follow WI 21 west for about 26.6 miles to the town of Redgranite. Turn right (northeast) on Division

The quarry is now a lake surrounded by large granite blocks from the quarry.

Street, and go about 0.2 mile. The former quarry, which is now a park, will be on the left.

Rockhounding

This is a former granite quarry that is now a 6-acre lake, and it has a maximum depth of 163 feet. It is owned by the Village of Redgranite and is open from 7 a.m to 7 p.m. With a name like Redgranite, I was hoping that the quarry would have some of the beautiful red granite that I have seen used for rip-rap and aggregate in parts of northern Wisconsin. Unfortunately, the granite is not red but a uniform fine-grained pinkish-gray granite. This was great for the quarry operators, as the stone was very consistent and predictable, but it is not a terribly exciting granite. The town should probably have been named "Pinkish-Gray Granite," but Redgranite sounded better to the village founders.

Although this is not really a red granite, the quarry is still worth a visit when in the region. The granite is well exposed and it is interesting to see

The quarry is a popular swimming hole, but unfortunately many people still drown in the quarry.

the large angular granite boulders that were mined and now placed along the lakeside and quarry highwalls. The granite is fine-grained and I did not see any indications of significant crystals, vugs, sulfides, other minerals, or pegmatites. I only got to visit the south side but I suspect the other areas of the quarry are similar, based on what I could see on the other side of the lake.

The lake has largemouth bass and pan fish, and reportedly also has trout and large catfish. The quarry is a popular swimming lake and sometimes has many people on the rocks and in the water. Unfortunately, many people have drowned in this lake. It is deep and the water is undoubtedly extremely cold once you reach the thermocline, even on the hottest summer days. I highly recommend looking at the quarry rocks when visiting Redgranite and forget about swimming in the lake.

Reference: Summers, 1965

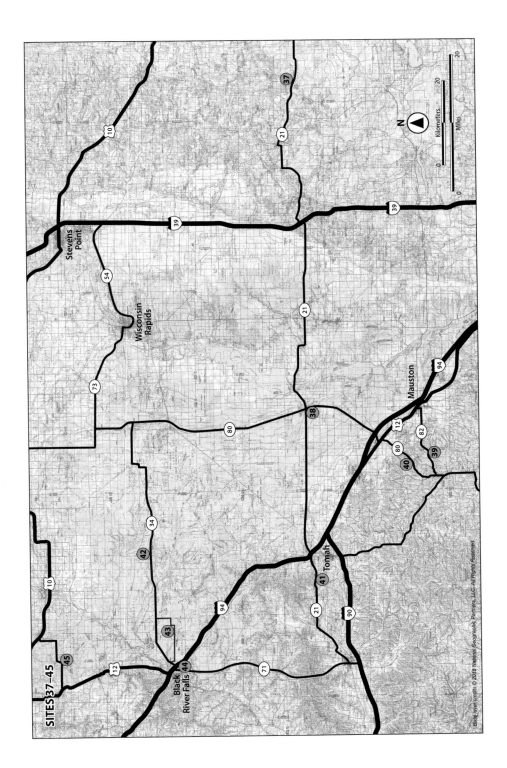

SITES 37–45

Stevens Point

Wisconsin Rapids

Mauston

Tomah

Black River Falls

38. Necedah Bluff Cambrian Sandstone and Quartz Crystals

The small quarry near the top of the bluff has lots of loose sandstone.

County: Juneau
Site type: Former Quarry
Land status: Vacant, undeveloped lots, not posted
Material: Quartzite with quartz crystals
Host rock: Precambrian quartzite
Difficulty: Easy
Family-friendly: Yes
Tools needed: Hammer
Special concerns: None
Special attractions: Rock climbing and hiking at nearby Petenwell Bluff
GPS parking: N44º 01.217' / W90º 04.733'
GPS quarry area: N44º 01.300' / W90º 04.617'

Many of the pieces have weathered sandstone that show the pattern of the quartz crystals.

Topographic quadrangle: Necedah, WI
Finding the site: Necedah is located between interstate highways I-94, I-90, and I-39, so your route to Necedah is dependent on which way you are approaching. From the closest interstate, I-90, take exit 61 to WI 80, and head north for 9.9 miles. WI 80 is also CR-A. Turn left (west) on 14th St as you reach Necedah. Continue 0.3 mile and turn right (north) on Precision Parkway, and go 0.6 mile. Turn left (west) onto West 6th St, and this turns into Oak Grove Drive. This goes west and then turns north. Take the first right and park at the barriers blocking the road. From here you can walk to the quarry and the rocks on top of Necedah Bluff.

Rockhounding

This is a former quarry near the top of Necedah Bluff. The rocks are a brecciated Precambrian quartzite. The quartzite is gray to light brown to pink, and the iron content varies throughout the quarry area. The quartzite has quite a bit of white vein quartz, but much of this is solid white quartz and does not contain crystals.

Small well-defined crystals of white quartz can be found loose on the ground.

The parking for this site is at a road built for what appears to be a future or failed housing development. The development has not yet been built, and fortunately I did not encounter any no trespassing signs or other indications that the area is closed. It is an easy walk up the hill to the large piles of quartzite. I was able to find some small quartz crystals fairly quickly among these piles. Most of the quartz crystals that I found were small. The best way to find the crystals is to search the loose piles of rock and look for indications of veins and cracks in the rock that may have opened some void spaces for crystals.

I later found out that I may have missed the main workings of the quarry. A quarry is on the southwest side of the hill, and this is readily seen on Google Maps. During my visit to this site I focused on the rocks on the hillside and the rocks that had quartz crystals. This goes to show how easy it can be to miss key features when they are obscured by trees. During future trips to this site I will be sure to look for the main quarry workings.

References: Brown et al. 1986; Cordua, 1998

39. Mauston Cambrian Sandstone Pseudo Fossils

The roadcut is easy to access but you must be careful of traffic.

County: Juneau
Site type: Roadcut
Land status: Not posted, likely in road right-of-way.
Material: Pseudo fossils
Host rock: Cambrian Sandstone and Dolostone
Difficulty: Easy
Family-friendly: Yes
Tools needed: Hammer
Special concerns: Traffic
Special attractions: None
GPS parking: N43° 46.467' / W90° 12.950'
Topographic quadrangle: New Lisbon South, WI

The pseudo fossils resemble small crinoids in cross section.

Finding the site: From I-94, take exit 69 to WI 82 west. Proceed nine miles to a long roadcut on the north side of WI 82. Park on the side of the road next to the roadcut.

Rockhounding

This is an accessible roadcut with an exposure of nearly horizontal Cambrian sandstone and dolostone. I had heard that some brachiopods could be found in a roadcut west of Mauston, and I stopped at this cut as parking and access were relatively easy.

I did not see any obvious fossils, but I came across some unusual features in the sandy zones of the roadcut that resembled crinoid columns in cross section. When I broke the rocks apart they resembled worm borrows. They were generally brown and lenticular, and at first I thought they might be a trace fossil. Trace fossils are common in many fossiliferous rocks, but sometimes it is not easy to tell the difference between a trace fossil and the actual creature that became a fossil.

The rocks are soft at this location and the best pseudo fossils are found in the loose rocks at the base of the cut.

The brown features I saw were found only in the sandstone sections of the roadcut. The sandstone was extremely soft and could easily be penetrated by the pick of my rock hammer. I later concluded that these could not be either trace fossils or actual fossils, as they could not be preserved in the soft sandstone. They must represent some other type of sedimentary structure. The best pieces seem to the loose pieces at the base of the cut that were hard enough to survive the rain and weathering. Since they could resemble fossils to a casual observer, I consider them to be "pseudo fossils." I have seen many other examples of pseudo fossils in sedimentary rocks. Strange features at the hand sample scale can form in sediments, so be careful before making too many conclusions about what a potential fossil may represent.

If you collect any of these pseudo fossils, keep in mind that they are very soft and can easily be damaged. Leaving them outside will result in rather quick erosion, and putting them with your other rocks will ensure that they are soon damaged. If you possibly have room for them in a display environment, that will be your best option.

Reference: USGS, 2004

40. Elroy Banded Cambrian Sandstones

This roadcut is covered with vegetation and is hard to see from the road.

County: Juneau
Site type: Roadcut
Land status: Not posted, likely in road right-of-way
Material: Banded and cross-bedded sandstones
Host rock: Cambrian Sandstone
Difficulty: Easy
Family-friendly: Yes
Tools needed: Hammer
Special concerns: Abundant vegetation obscures outcrops
Special attractions: None
GPS parking: N43° 48.733' / W90° 14.050'
Topographic quadrangle: New Lisbon South, WI

The sandstone shows excellent banding and is generally light gray to brown.

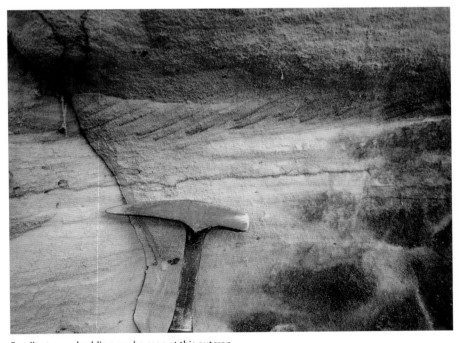

Excellent cross-bedding can be seen at this outcrop.

Finding the site: From WI 71 in Elroy, turn north on WI 80 Trunk North, which is also known as Academy Road. Continue north for 6 miles, and look a small unpaved driveway on the west side of WI 80. Park here, taking care to not block any other users of the driveway. Walk southward on WI 80, being extremely careful of the traffic. The roadcut is just south of the guardrails and is on the west side of the road.

Rockhounding

I had stopped for fossils at this location, but the exposure was entirely sandstone and I did not see any fossils. However, the sandstone here is colorful and has some attractive iron-rich bands. The sandstone also has some excellent cross-bedding.

Most of the sandstone is soft but there are some harder sections as well. The best way to collect intact pieces is to knock off a section and break it apart with your hammer. Although the overall sandstone is soft it is easy to break off the better cemented pieces. Many of these have strong banding. The color of the sandstone at this location ranges from white to orange to dark brown to purple.

Reference: USGS, 2004

41. Tunnel City Sandstone

County: Monroe
Site type: Roadcut
Land status: Not posted, likely road right-of-way
Material: Gray sandstone with crossbeds
Host rock: Cambrian Sandstones
Difficulty: Easy
Family-friendly: Yes
Tools needed: Hammer
Special concerns: Traffic, limited parking
Special attractions: None
GPS parking: N44º 00.567' / W90º 34.650'
Topographic quadrangle: Tunnel City, WI
Finding the site: From I-94, take exit 143 to WI 21. Continue until you hit US 12, which is North Superior Avenue. From the intersection of WI 21 and US 12, continue 3.7 miles. The roadcut will be on the right (north) side of the road. Park on the shoulder of WI 21. I parked on the south side of the highway just east of the guardrail.

Rockhounding

This is a roadcut in gray Cambrian sandstone. Based on the proximity to Tunnel City, I am assuming this is the Tunnel City sandstone. This site is unique as it is just north of a mine operated by Unimin. This mine produces industrial sand, and much of this sand is used for hydraulic fracturing of oil and gas well. The well-sorted and rounded character of early Paleozoic sandstones make them economic for use as industrial sand. Many sands that formed in later geologic periods often do not have the correct size, roundness, and hardness that are found in early Paleozoic sandstones.

I was able to access this roadcut very easily. The sandstone is generally light to dark gray, and has well-defined crossbeds. I thought that when I broke a piece off the roadcut that I would see white sandstone. Instead, I found that the interior of the sandstone was dark gray. The dark gray may be due to glauconite in this sandstone. Glauconite is an iron potassium phyllosilicate. It is an authigenic mineral, which means that it formed after the original sandstone was deposited. It forms exclusively in marine sediments and typically forms under low oxygen conditions. Glauconite is not weather-resistant and it tends to break down when exposed on fresh surfaces.

The sandstones show excellent crossbeds.

The glauconite is interesting, but I thought the most intriguing aspect of this cut is the crossbeds in the sandstone. While crossbeds are common in many sandstone roadcuts in Wisconsin, the beds here are generally between eye-level and waist-level so you can observe the crossbeds and sandstone mineralogy closely.

The sandstone at this site is very soft and it is difficult to find durable pieces. If you collect sandstone at this site, be sure to keep it in dry place away from wind and rain. Further exposure to rain and wind causes this sandstone to break apart, so this sandstone is definitely not the kind of rock you would like to keep outside.

References: Twenhofel, 1936; USGS, 2004

42. Saddle Mound Trace Fossils and Sandstone

These trace fossils are on the top of the ridge at the base of a railing on the ridgeline trail.

County: Jackson County
Site type: Hilltop and hillside exposures
Land status: Uncertain, not posted
Material: Trace fossils and Sandstone
Host rock: Cambrian Sandstone
Difficulty: Easy
Family-friendly: Yes
Tools needed: Hammer
Special concerns: Strenuous climb to top of Saddle Mound
Special attractions: Wazee Lake Recreation Area
GPS parking: N44° 20.833' / W90° 30.333'
Trace Fossils on Ridge: N44° 20.983' / W90° 30.017'
Topographic quadrangle: Hatfield SE, WI

The sandstone is nearly all quartz but does have minor limonitic bands.

Finding the site: From I-94, take exit 115 to WI 54. Proceed 16.9 miles, and turn left on Saddle Mound Road. Proceed about 0.4 mile, and park on the southwest (left) side of the road. This will be opposite a small sandy road that leads toward the top of Saddle Mount. This road is very sandy and I highly recommend walking to make sure you do not get stuck in the sand.

Rockhounding

Saddle Mound is a prominent hill of Cambrian sandstone. The hill had two sandstone quarries during the nineteenth and early twentieth centuries, and photographs of the workings show that much of the mound was stripped of trees during the working of the quarries. Today the area is covered with woods, and footpaths lead to the top of Saddle Mound. A fire tower is near the top of the summit.

   I parked on the west side of Saddle Mound Road and hiked on the entrance road in the direction of the summit. This road soon converged with another road and then to a road that eventually became a trail. These roads have wash outs and are best suited for hiking, not driving. The trail rapidly became very steep and I was surprised at the level of effort needed to reach the top. As I climbed the mound I saw many excellent cross-bedded sandstones, and I saw some steep cliffs that I assumed where the former highwalls of the quarrying operation. They were too steep and too overgrown with trees and brush to get a closer look. The best option was to stay on the trail.

Once you reach the top, which is on the western end of Saddle Mound, the hiking is much easier as you are now on the ridge. I walked eastward and soon came to a metal railing that had been placed were the trail began to descend. I assume this might have been installed after the quarrying ended and it was a rail for hikers. Near this rail on the ground is a flat area with hard, light-colored sandstone that has trace fossils. These resemble worm tracks or burrows. They are subject to lots of foot traffic and are best left undisturbed by hammering so other visitors can see them. I looked for other rocks in the area with trace fossils but did not see any. I am sure there are likely more in this area.

As I continued my descent, which was much easier than climbing on the east side, I came across some open areas that apparently had been mined. Some of these had outcrops of white and light orange sandstone, and these had excellent bands of limonite and cross-bedding. This is a great place to see sandstone in a previous quarry operation.

On another note, this is a tick-infested area, like many parts of Wisconsin. I was there in late May 2017. As I continued down the trail I counted six ticks at once crawling up my pants legs, despite all the insect repellent I used. Ticks are one of the hazards that we face in this hobby and you always have to be aware when they are out and ready to get you.

References: Brown, 1983; Hess et al., 2017; USGS, 2004

43. Black River Falls Iron Mine

County: Jackson
Site type: Former iron mine
Land status: Wazee Lake Recreation Area
Material: Magnetite, hematite, garnet, actinolite, malachite
Host rock: Precambrian banded iron formation beneath Cambrian sediments
Difficulty: Easy
Family-friendly: Yes
Tools needed: None
Special concerns: Collecting not allowed, area is now a park
Special attractions: Wazee Lake
GPS parking (mineralized area): N44° 17.817' / W90° 43.967'
Topographic quadrangle: Hatfield SW, WI
Finding the site: From I-94, take exit 116 to WI 82, and head northeast. Go approximately 0.4 mile, and turn right onto West Bauer Road. Go 3.8 miles, and turn right (south) onto North Brockway Road. Go 0.2 mile, and turn left (east) onto Wazee Lake Road. Go 0.6 mile and you will then enter the park. Turn left on the road after the park entrance. Go 0.3 mile, and turn left onto an unnamed road, and then take a sharp left. Continue about 0.4 mile, and then turn left (south) onto another unnamed road. Continue about 500 feet, and park here. The mineralized rocks are in the broad swale to the southeast. These are readily apparent on satellite photos of the area.

Rockhounding

The former Black River Falls iron mine was an open pit mine that operated from 1969 to about 1983. Iron was first mined in the Black River Falls area in the mid-nineteenth century near Tilden Mound just north of the town of Black River Falls. However, the ore was low-grade and no significant iron mines were developed.

Around 1940, Inland Steel began acquiring land and mining rights in the area. The Chicago-based company needed a year-round source of iron, as their iron sources in the Lake Superior region were often not accessible during the winter. They finally received company approval to develop the Black River Falls mine in 1967. The demand for American steel was still strong, but many steel companies were already beginning to suffer from high production costs and increased competition from overseas. Although the mine was developed

This rock is rich in magnetite and is common in this part of the former mine.

into a large open pit and still had at least ten years left of reserves, Inland Steel decided to close the mine in 1982. The huge pumps that kept the mine dry were turned off, and within two years the mine became a large lake.

The former mine area is now the Wazee Lake Recreation Area, which is a Jackson County Park. Like many lakes from the open pits of former iron mines that had primarily magnetite and hematite ores, the water in the lake is remarkably clear. The lake is popular with scuba divers and it is the deepest water body in the interior of Wisconsin.

While it is great that the former mine is now open to the public, collecting is not allowed in the park. However, there are no restrictions on looking at the mineralized rocks. The access roads have many large rocks that line the roadsides, but most of these are gneissic rocks that do not contain many interesting mineral. The best place that I found to see mineralized rocks are in the broad grassy area west of the lake and south of the road. This area has abundant magnetite, hematite, garnet, actinolite, and some minor malachite. Some of the garnet is in schistose rocks and occurs as reddish porphyroblasts in a matrix of fine-grained muscovite. The magnetite-rich rocks are extremely dense

This is a foliated schist that is rich in garnet and chlorite.

and loaded with iron. This would have been a fascinating mine to collect in when it was operating.

Another great place to see some mineralized rocks is at the former tailings pond. This is north of Wazee Lake and road signs in the park can lead you to it. This is a large pond, but it is small when compared to Lake Wazee. Near the entrance road to the pond there are some large piles of mine rocks, and some of these have magnetite, hematite, and other minerals associated with the former mine.

Ironically, when compared to other iron mines, the Black River Falls Iron Mine was small. If you have the opportunity to visit this site you may not think it was small. To me, Lake Wazee looked very large, and it is hard to believe that this lake was the site of an iron mine just over 30 years ago.

References: Hess and Hess, 2017; Kimball and Spear, 1984; USGS, 2004

44. Black River Falls Precambrian Granite

County: Jackson
Site type: River bed below dam
Land status: Public access as a portage trail is on east bank
Material: Granite
Host rock: Precambrian Granite
Difficulty: Easy
Family-friendly: Yes
Tools needed: None
Special concerns: Dam has lots of warnings about water release
Special attractions: Wazee Lake
GPS parking: N44° 17.800' / W90° 50.620'
GPS river bed: N44° 17.783' / W90° 50.680'
Topographic quadrangle: Black River Falls, WI
Finding the site: From I-94 at the town of Black River Falls, take exit 116, and head west on WI 54, which is also East Main Street. Continue for 1.1 miles, and turn right (north) onto Cedar Street. Go 0.2 mile and turn left (west) onto North Roosevelt Road. Go about 200 feet and park in the small parking lot on the left (south) side of the road. From here you can walk to the dam site and follow the path to the rocks in the river bed.

Rockhounding

The granite at Black River Falls is a Middle to Late Proterozoic granite that intruded Archean gneisses. The granite is largely undeformed and does not exhibit many indications of strain in the rocks.

The granite is well exposed below the dam. The granite is generally a pinkish-gray to red, but it does not have an abundance of red granite. Many of the rocks have a light coat of fine brown river sediment so it is difficult to see the original color of the granite. The large boulders are too smooth and massive to break off pieces to see a fresh surface, but there are many small rocks that can be broken with a hammer, if you decide to bring one to this site.

A path below the dam is used as a portage trail for canoeists. The dam has a warning sign indicating that a turbine discharge area is below the dam. You must exit immediately for higher ground if you hear the warning horn. The

The granite is extremely hard and uniform throughout the river bed.

dam also has a sign that indicates no fishing, no diving, no motor boats, and no swimming. This sign also tells people to stay on the path. Fortunately, there are no signs that specifically prohibit rockhounding, but it is still probably a good idea to stay close to the shore and minimize any hammering that you may choose to do.

Reference: Brown, 1983

45. Wildcat Mound Giraffe Rock

The cliffs at Wildcat Mound are sheer faces with drops of more than 100 feet.

County: Clark
Site type: Cliffs along trail
Land status: County Park
Material: "Giraffe" pattern sandstone, locally known as zebra rock
Host rock: Cambrian sandstone
Difficulty: Easy
Family-friendly: Yes
Tools needed: None
Special concerns: Snakes and cliffs
Special attractions: None
GPS parking: N44° 31.567' / W90° 48.633'
GPS outcrops: N44° 31.367' / W90° 48.433'
Topographic quadrangle: Wildcat Mound, WI

The sandstone is white and often mottled with orange.

Finding the site: From I-94 near Black River Falls, take exit 115 to US 12. This is the same highway as WI 27. Continue north for 20.3 miles to Humbird, and then turn right (east) onto CR-B. Proceed 3.9 miles to the entrance to Wildcat Mound Park. To get to the trailhead, follow the park road about 500 feet to the southwest to a parking area. Park here, and follow the trail up the mound. The trail curves around the mound to the east, and the best outcrops are on the southern side of Wildcat Mound.

Rockhounding

This is one of the best exposures of banded Cambrian sandstones that I have seen in Wisconsin. The outcrops are known locally as "zebra rock" and I expected to see horizontal bands of black and white. My wife and I took this hike, and she said that it did not look like zebra banding. The rocks were not banded in black and white as much as they were mottled orange and white. My wife said the rocks resembled the pattern on a giraffe much more than a zebra, so we called this "giraffe rock."

This is a Clark County park, and to the credit of Clark County management, they do not charge a fee to visit this park like many other county parks

Nearly everyone that has seen this photo calls the stone "giraffe" rock and not zebra rock.

in Wisconsin. They recognize that it is better to let us spend that fee back into the local economy and the park will certainly get more visitors. It was refreshing to not see another self-service fee bin.

I had reviewed the area on a topographic map so I knew the correct way to find the exposures was to follow the trail southwest from the parking lot, and it would then curve toward the east around Wildcat Mound. We hiked up a moderately steep trail, which had some large wooden railroad ties for steps. Quickly the trail levelled out and we were soon walking along the sandstone that was deposited in the Cambrian.

It was a hot September day, and the sandstone cliffs made me feel like we were in the American southwest desert instead of central Wisconsin. The scenery was very impressive, and the weather was perfect. However, we soon got a shock that reversed the mood of this so-far perfect trip.

I saw a large, orange-and-brown snake on one of the rocks. It was about 4 feet long. The head was narrow, and I assumed it was nonvenomous. However, it still shook up my wife. Almost immediately afterward I found another snake sunning itself on the rocks. This one was brown and gray, and had a bigger, triangular head. I then saw it began to coil and rattle its tail, even though it did not have any rattles. That was enough for me. We backed away and continued along the trail, which had now become rocky.

My wife then said, "Hey, you walked right by one." I had walked right next to a 4-foot snake. If so inclined, it could have easily struck me. I then realized that we might have a problem here. The place might be a massive snake den. I thought of Samuel L. Jackson's quote from *Snakes on a Plane* but cannot repeat that here. We both got large sticks just to help us check over rocks as we walked on the trail. We had no intention of hurting or disturbing any snakes, and wanted to make sure we did not surprise any that were along the trail.

We continued our hike and found that the best exposures of the giraffe rock are toward the eastern end of the cliffs. There are many loose rocks on the ground, and you do not want to dig in the cliffs. Unfortunately there is quite a bit of graffiti and initials in the soft sandstone. We followed the trail to where the cliffs ended, then came to a fork. One went up the hill to the top of the cliffs, and the other likely went in a big circle back to the parking lot. We took the route to the top of the cliffs, and eventually followed a trail back to the parking lot. We did not see any more snakes. The cliffs offer an excellent view to the south, but you must stay away from the edge.

This is a great trip but you have to be aware of the potential for snakes. The cliffs are also dangerous on top, but you will be fine as long as you stay away from the edge. After this trip, I will be careful about other mounds we visit. Wisconsin has a mound called "Rattlesnake Mound" and I am going to stay away from that one.

References: Klemick and Ohlson, 1973; USGS, 2004; IMDb, 2017

46. Big Falls Hornblende Gneiss

Banded gneiss is well exposed and polished at Big Falls, which is a popular falls on the Eau Claire River.

County: Eau Claire
Site type: River bank outcrops and loose rocks
Land status: County Park
Material: Hornblende Gneiss
Host rock: Precambrian metagabbro
Difficulty: Easy
Family-friendly: Yes
Tools needed: None
Special concerns: Slippery rocks near falls
Special attractions: None
GPS parking: N44° 49.183' / W91° 17.433'
GPS outcrops: N44° 49.267' / W91° 17.533'
Topographic quadrangle: Fall Creek, WI

This loose piece of hornblende gneiss was found in the gneiss outcrop just south and west of Big Falls.

Finding the site: From I-94, take exit 81 north, and then turn right (east) onto CR-HH. Go 2.2 miles and turn left (north) onto CR-KK. Go 11.9 miles north, and then turn left (west) onto Big Falls Forest Road. Proceed 1.0 mile to the parking area for the trail to the falls. Park here, and be sure to pay the self-service county park fee before leaving your car. Walk about 1000 feet to the falls. The hornblende gneiss is in an outcrop on the south bank just downstream of the falls.

Rockhounding

Big Falls is a waterfall on the Eau Claire River that flows over a large exposure of Archean metagabbro and associated gneisses. The rocks are Archean and are among the older Precambrian rocks in the region. The gneiss has been polished by the river, and there are surprisingly few rocks by the falls. The gneiss has an excellent banded appearance but the individual minerals are small and it is relatively fine-grained.

To get to the hornblende gneiss you have to walk downstream of the falls on the south side of the bank. You will soon see some outcrops of white and

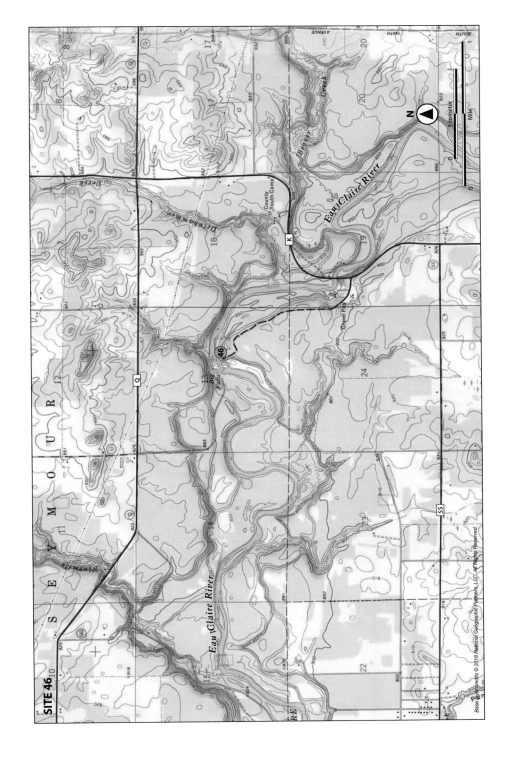

SITE 46

This is the site with the hornblende gneiss, and loose pieces are easy to find in this area.

gray rocks on the river bank. Look closely and you will see that many of these rocks are rich in black hornblende. The hornblende occurs as coarse bladed crystals and is set in a light gray matrix of plagioclase feldspar. The black crystals in the white matrix is quite striking.

The hornblende gneiss is confined to this immediate area. We walked downstream to find more exposures but the rocks were either covered by river sediments or woods. A review of the satellite photos of the area also suggests that other outcrops are not in the immediate area downstream, so your time is likely best spent at the hornblende gneiss outcrop and relaxing by the falls.

References: Myers et al., 1974; Cummings, 1984; Sims, 1990; USGS, 2004

NORTHERN HIGHLAND

47. Quiver Falls Precambrian Metabasalt

The basalt is dark green and pillow basalts are reported in this area.

County: Marinette
Site type: Exposure along river
Land status: Menominee River State Recreation Area
Material: Dark green metabasalt of Quinnesec Formation
Host rock: Early Proterozoic mafic metavolcanic rocks
Difficulty: Easy
Family-friendly: No
Tools needed: None
Special concerns: Steep slopes, must be careful near river
Special attractions: None
GPS parking: N45º 39.283' / W87º 49.633'
GPS outcrop: N45º 39.250' / W87º 49.617'

Topographic quadrangle: Faithorn, WI-MI
Finding the site: From US 8 in Pembine, take CR-R, which becomes Kremlin Road, east for 7.5 miles. Take the right fork to Pembine Dam Road, go 0.1 mile, and turn left (northeast) onto Pemene Dam Road after you cross some railroad tracks. Continue on Pemene Dam Road for 0.8 mile. You will then arrive at a kiosk. Drive down the road to the right to the parking area, and then hike to the river. This location is a canoe launching point and has excellent access.

Rockhounding

This is a scenic site next to Menominee River. Quiver Falls is better described as a whitewater rapid, and some guides do not consider it to be a real waterfall. Unfortunately, the trails were a little confusing and we did not get to walk to Quiver Falls as the slopes appeared to steep. Instead, we reached the river by going to a canoe launching site just south of the rapids.

The outcrops are on the western side of the Menominee River near the canoe launching location. There are other outcrops further upstream but access is difficult due to the steep cliffs. The area at the canoe launching site is not as steep and it is easy to hike on the slopes. This area has dark green metabasalt exposed on the hillsides.

Pillow basalts are reported to be in this area. Pillow basalts are basalts that erupted underwater and cooled quickly on all sides. This results in a "pillow" appearance. I did not see any pillows but it was hard to see exposures due to the trees and ground cover. Freshly broken surfaces of the basalt are generally dark green, and some light green sections are also present. Closer inspection of the area would likely reveal some pillow basalts, as well as other minerals and features, such as varioles, associated with metabasalts.

References: Sims et al., 1992; Schulz and LaBerge, 2003

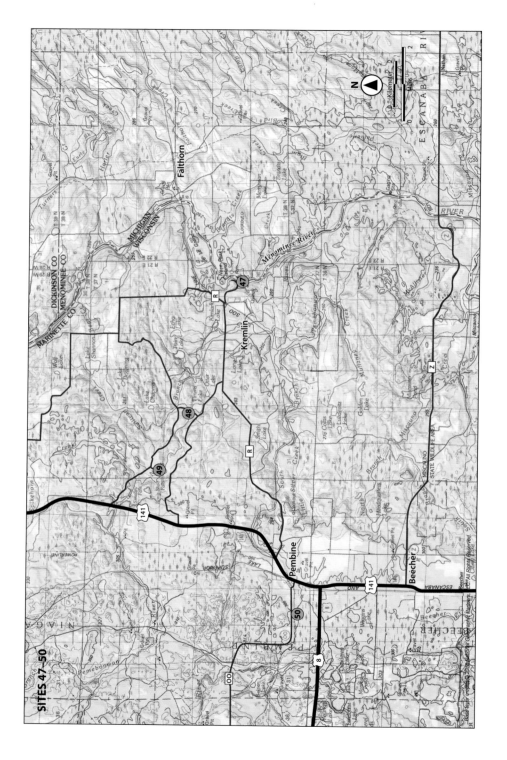

SITES 47–50

48. Pemebonwon River Precambrian Metabasalt

This is the southern outcrop of the basalt near the River.

County: Marinette
Site type: Roadcut
Land status: Likely highway right of way, not posted
Material: Dark green metabasalt
Host rock: Early Proterozoic mafic metavolcanic rocks
Difficulty: Easy
Family-friendly: Yes
Tools needed: None
Special concerns: Traffic
Special attractions: None
GPS parking: N45° 40.367 ' / W87° 53.917'
Topographic quadrangle: Pembine, WI

This is the northern outcrop of the basalt near the River, and this basalt has more loose rocks.

Finding the site: From US 8 in Pembine, take CR-R, which becomes Kremlin Road, east for 5.0 miles. Turn left (north) onto Timms Lake Road. Continue 1.3 miles, and turn right onto Morgan Lake Road. Go 0.3 mile and park on the east side of the road and just south of the Pemebonwon River. The roadcuts are on the west side of the road south of the river and on the east side of the road north of the river.

Rockhounding

This site has two roadcuts that expose dark green metabasalt. The exposure are on both sides of Pemebonwon River. The basalt is similar at each roadcut, but the northern exposure is more fractured and has many more hand-sized pieces.

These outcrops are listed here as they are easily accessed and well-exposed examples of Precambrian metabasalt. Unfortunately, I did not see any significant mineralization or pillow basalts at this location. However, it would still be worthwhile to explore these outcrops in greater detail. At a minimum you can get some good pieces of green metabasalt.

References: Sims et al., 1992

49. Long Slide Falls Precambrian Greenschist

Long Slide Falls descends 50 feet in a long cascade over the more resistant rocks of the area.

County: Marinette
Site type: Rocks along waterfall
Land status: Long Slide Falls County Park
Material: Greenschist
Host rock: Early Proterozoic mafic metavolcanic rocks
Difficulty: Easy
Family-friendly: Yes
Tools needed: None
Special concerns: Must be careful around falls, moderately steep hike
Special attractions: Other Marinette County waterfalls
GPS parking: N45° 41.100' / W87° 55.950'
GPS falls: N45° 41.000' / W87° 55.967'

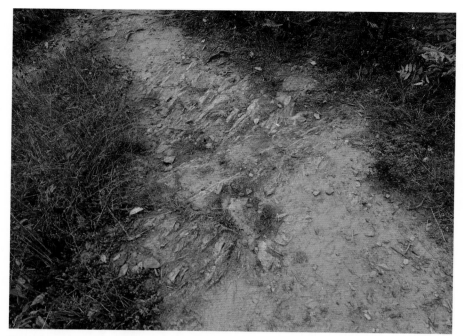

The rocks are best exposed on the trail and are light green, platy, weakly foliated rocks best described as a greenschist.

Topographic quadrangle: Pembine, WI
Finding the site: From US 8 in Pembine, take US 141/8 north for 5.5 miles. Turn right (east) onto Morgan Park Road, and continue east for 1.6 miles. Turn right (south) onto Lone Slide Road, and continue 0.3 mile to the parking area. Pay the county park fee and hike to the falls.

Rockhounding

Long Slide Falls is one of many waterfalls in Marinette County, and some guides say this is the most impressive falls in northeastern Wisconsin. This is a long slide over hundreds of feet, and the falls descend about 50 feet over their length. The trail from the parking lot splits into two, with the west trail leading to the falls, and the east trail leading to the area below the falls. The best rocks and best view of the falls are seen by taking the east trail that descends to the base of the falls. This is a moderately steep hike and you should be careful if the rocks are wet.

The rocks are best described as a hard, fine-grained greenschist, and are in an area mapped as mafic metavolcanic rocks. The rocks are moderately foliated and do not have any individual minerals visible in hand sample. The falls cut into the rocks but they are still resistant enough to form the long slide of the water fall. The rocks have a platy character, and on some sections of the trails to the falls they resemble light green serpentine. When the rocks are broken many are crystalline inside, and they are not soft like serpentine. The green color appears to be from fine-grained chlorite. Many of the best rocks are found loose on the trail as you descend to the area below the falls. The best view of the falls is also from downstream.

References: Sims et al., 1992

50. Pembine Tonalite

County: Marinette
Site type: Outcrops adjacent to railroad
Land status: Land adjacent to railroad
Material: Tonalite
Host rock: Early Proterozoic tonalite of the Pembine-Wausau Terrane
Difficulty: Moderate
Family-friendly: No, hike may be too long
Tools needed: Hammer
Special concerns: Must be careful walking near tracks
Special attractions: None
GPS parking: N45° 37.983' / W87° 59.750'
GPS outcrop: N45° 37.600' / W88° 00.650'
Topographic quadrangle: Dunbar NE, WI
Finding the site: From the intersection of US 8 and US 141, take US 141 north for 0.7 mile, then turn left (west) onto Elm Street. Proceed 0.2 mile. After you cross the railroad, park on the right (east) side of the road. From here, walk about 1 mile west to the outcrops on the north side of the railroad.

Rockhounding

Like roadcuts, exposures along railroads often provide good opportunities to see rocks. However, you must always be extremely careful around active rail lines. This exposure at this site requires a hike of approximately 1 mile to the outcrops, but fortunately the railroad at this area is double-tracked and very wide.

The rock at this site is described as tonalite, which is a quartz-rich intrusive rock where plagioclase makes up greater than 90 percent of the feldspar in the rock. The tonalite exposures are not large but are easy to find on the north side of the railroad. There are two exposures in the same general area. The western outcrop, which is the largest, is just north of a sign that says "RXR 1 MILE." Note that this sign also faces west, so you will not see the writing when approaching from the east. The eastern outcrop is a little smaller and is about 300 feet to the east of the western outcrop.

Information on this area indicated that the tonalite had blue quartz, but much to my disappointment I could not see any blue quartz in hand sample. The tonalite is fine-grained and rich in quartz and white feldspar, which

The tonalite is fine-grained and is reported to have blue quartz, but I could not find any blue quartz in hand samples.

I assume is plagioclase, given the composition of tonalite. This rock is different from the other intrusive rocks of the area as it is fine-grained, and while rich in quartz, most of the feldspar is white plagioglase instead of the orange potassium feldspar found in many of the granitic rocks in Wisconsin. While it is fine-grained it is still phaneritic and you can see the individual quartz and feldspar grains. It would be interesting to view this in thin section and see if the quartz is indeed blue when seen under a microscope.

References: Cordua, 1998; Sims et al., 1992

51. Niagara Railroad Cut Precambrian Granite

The cuts are well exposed along the rail line.

County: Marinette

Site type: Railroad Cut

Land status: Railroad

Material: Granite with dark red feldspars

Host rock: Early Proterozoic Quinnesec Formation gneiss and granite

Difficulty: Easy

Family-friendly: No

Tools needed: Hammer

Special concerns: Must stay off railroad tracks

Special attractions: Iron Mountain Iron Mine Tour in Michigan

GPS parking: N45° 46.083' / W88° 02.800'

GPS north outcrop (pegmatite): N45° 46.373' / W88° 02.978'

GPS south outcrop (granite): N45° 46.282' / W88° 02.875'

The granite in the southern cut is coarse-grained and has white and dark orange feldspar.

Topographic quadrangle: Iron Mountain, WI-MI
Finding the site: From the intersection of US 141 and CR-N in Niagara, take CR-N 2.0 miles to a railroad crossing. Park on the north side of road, and walk approximately one-third of a mile to the outcrops on the side of the railroad. The northern outcrop has coarse minerals that may be part of a small pegmatite, and the southern outcrop has the granite with dark red feldspars.

Rockhounding

This is a couple of small outcrops just north of CR–N on a rail line. I visited the site late on a weekend afternoon in June 2012 and did not have any issues with trains, but you must be extremely careful whenever collecting near railroads. The outcrops are reported to have a shear zone with fluorite, but I did not encounter any fluorite. The northern outcrop has a small coarse-grained dike that resembles a pegmatite, but the rocks at the outcrop were extremely hard and difficult to break off the outcrop.

The southern outcrop is more interesting. It has some coarse-grained granite with deep red feldspars, which contrast well with the light gray to

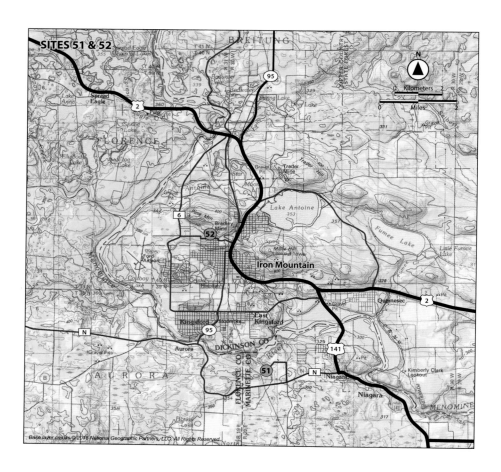

light orange feldspars, gray quartz, and dark minerals, which I assume are biotite or hornblende. This outcrop is very different from the outcrops with iron-rich minerals in the area and is worth a stop if you are in this part of northern Marinette County.

References: Cordua, 1998; Sims et al., 1992

52. Bradley Iron Mine Hematite and Iron Formation

County: Dickinson (Michigan)

Site type: Mine dump of former iron mine

Land status: Uncertain, not posted

Material: Specular hematite, banded iron formation

Host rock: Precambrian Vulcan Iron Formation

Difficulty: Easy

Family-friendly: Yes, dump is right next to parking area

Tools needed: Hammer

Special concerns: Land status uncertain

Special attractions: Iron Mountain Iron Mine Tour in Vulcan, Michigan

GPS parking: N45° 49.583' / W88° 04.433'

Topographic quadrangle: Iron Mountain, WI-MI

Finding the site: From US 2/141 in Iron Mountain, take Kent Street west for 0.3 mile. Turn right (north) onto Fairbanks Street. Continue for 0.2 mile to North Foster Street and turn right (north). Continue north about 300 feet, and North Foster Street becomes Walker Street and turns left (west). Park on the shoulder of the road. You will be able to see a large mine dump from the Bradley mine just north of Walker Street.

Rockhounding

The Bradley iron mine is shown on the USGS topographic map for Iron Mountain, WI-MI. It is just west of the pit for the Chapin Mine, which was the largest iron ore producer in the Menominee Iron–Bearing District. The Bradley mine is one of the younger mines in the district as it opened in 1937 and continued operating until at least the 1960s. In contrast, the Chapin mine opened in 1880 and closed in 1934.

The Bradley mine is surrounded by a fence and access is not possible without permission. However, there is a large mine dump outside of the fenced area on the north side of Walker Street. I visited this area in 2012 and 2016. The first time I visited the site in 2012 at least three deer were next to the mine dump. I found some excellent fine-grained specular hematite and

The dump has abundant specular hematite and iron formation in loose pieces on the ground.

banded iron formation. The second time I visited the site in 2016 I did not see any deer, but I found that the mine dump was nearly the same. It was still easy to find good iron formation and specular hematite. This site is easy to find and access, and it is worth a stop when in the Iron Mountain area.

References: Bayley et al., 1966

53. Pine River Power Plant Slate

Pine River can be viewed from the power plant catwalk, and a large outcrop of slate can be seen in the lower left of this photo.

County: Marinette
Site type: Outcrops on river bank
Land status: Power plant, public access
Material: Slate
Host rock: Early Proterozoic Michagamme Formation of the Baraga Group
Difficulty: Easy
Family-friendly: Yes
Tools needed: Hammer
Special concerns: Must be careful near river and power plant
Special attractions: Fishing in Pine River Flowage
GPS parking: N45° 49.600' / W88° 14.900'
GPS outcrops: N45° 49.600' / W88° 14.850'
Topographic quadrangle: Iron Mountain SW, WI-MI

The slate cleaves into flat pieces and tiny dark red garnets can be found on the surface of some of the slate.

Finding the site: From the intersection of CR-N and CR-B west of Aurora, go west on CR-N for 5.1 miles. Turn right (north) at the intersection with CR-C to stay north, and continue for 1.7 miles. Turn left (west) onto Power Dam Road, go 1.3 miles, then keep right to stay on Power Dam Road. Proceed 0.4 mile to the parking area. From here, hike down to the Pine River and look for outcrops of slate near the river bank.

Rockhounding

The Pine River Power Plant is located downstream of the dam for the Pine River Flowage. The power house was built in 1922 and is operated by Wisconsin Electric Power. The Power Plant has a walkway that allows you to walk around the plant and you can get an excellent downstream view of the Pine River from the plant walkway.

The slate outcrops are on the south side of the Pine River just downstream of the Power Plant. The slate is within the Michagamme Formation of

An outcrop with broken slate is present near the trail on the south side of the Pine River east of the power plant.

the Baraga Group, and it is Early Proterozoic. The slate is dark gray and well bedded, and generally cleaves into pieces that are ¼ to ½ inch thick. Tiny dark red garnets can be seen on the surfaces of the slates in some areas of the outcrop. While the garnets are very small, the slate is hard and can be split into large flat pieces.

References: Dutton, 1971; Cannon, 1986; USGS, 2004

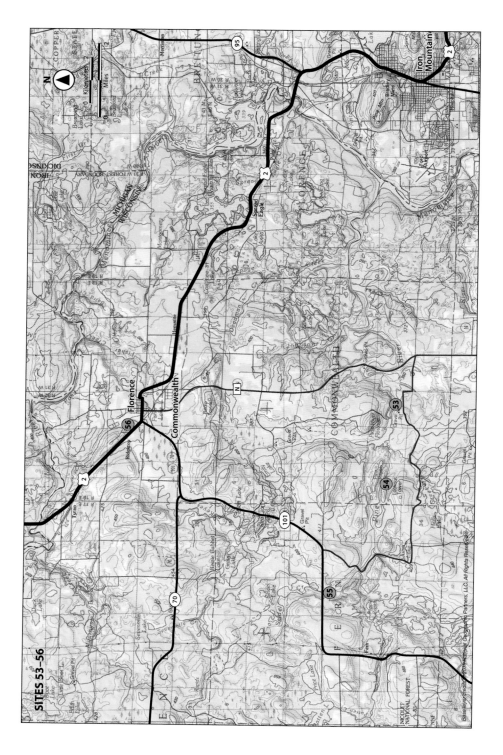

SITES 53–56

54. LaSalle Falls Black Tourmaline

This schist has a small crystalline black mineral that may be black tourmaline.

County: Florence
Site type: Outcrops near waterfall
Land status: Pine Popple Wild Rivers (State of Wisconsin)
Material: Black tourmaline
Host rock: Early Proterozoic mafic metavolcanic rocks
Difficulty: Moderate
Family-friendly: Yes
Tools needed: None, Wild Rivers Property
Special concerns: Falls are dangerous, stay away from cliff and stream bank
Special attractions: LaSalle Falls
GPS parking: N45° 49.283' / W88° 17.250'
GPS falls outcrops: N45° 49.850' / W88° 17.400'

GPS CR-C outcrops: N45° 47.983' / W88° 15.417'
Topographic quadrangle: Florence SE, WI
Finding the site: From the intersection of WI 101 and CR-C in the small town of Fence, take CR-C 10.0 miles to LaSalle Falls Road. The turnoff to LaSalle Falls Road is marked with a sign. Drive 2.4 miles on LaSalle Falls Road to the turnoff for the parking area, which will be on your right (north). Park here and follow the trail north for approximately 1 mile to the falls. The tourmaline-bearing rocks are in the dark schist outcrops near the trail at the falls. Another outcrop that is worth visiting is the graffiti-covered gneissic schist just west of the intersection of LaSalle Falls and CR-C.

Rockhounding

LaSalle Falls is a waterfall on the Pine River. It is better described as a "slide" as the falls are much longer than their height. They have a total drop of only 22 feet but the canyon and the volume of water makes them seem much larger. The falls are considered to be one of the most scenic of the region, and are reached by a moderate hike from a parking area at the trailhead.

The falls are near the contact of mafic metavolcanics on the south side of the river and metamorphosed dacite and volcanic greywacke on the north side of the river. All the rocks in the area are Early Proterozoic in age. The falls formed over a resistant rhyolitic breccia, and the river cut through a more easily eroded unit of sulfide-bearing schist below the falls.

I have been to the site twice, and the trail ends above the falls. The outcrops above the falls, which are sparse and covered with moss and soil, are generally dark schists. Some of these have splays of black tourmaline crystals. These are hard to find as there are no fresh cuts of rock in this area. You have to look closely on broken pieces of the schists.

Despite being at the site twice, I was not able to find the trail down to view the falls from the bottom of Pine Creek. During both visits I was with my family and it would not have been possible for them to climb into the gorge with me, so I cannot report on what I found below the falls. However, based on descriptions of the geology of the falls, it seems reasonable to assume that pyrite could be found in the rhyolitic rocks below the falls.

On our way out we also stopped at the outcrop that is just west of the intersection of LaSalle Falls Road and CR-C. This outcrop is covered with

The graffiti-covered outcrop has some schistose zones with abundant parallel black minerals, which appear to be hornblende.

graffiti, so it is hard to miss. The outcrop is mainly gneiss but there is a part that is more schistose and covered with fine-grained mica and dark minerals that are oriented parallel to the foliation. Based on their abundance and overall appearance I assume they are hornblendes.

References: Schulz and LaBerge, 2003

55. Pine River Red Tourmaline

The outcrop with the tourmaline-bearing pegmatites is in the woods west of Pine River and can be hard to find.

County: Florence
Site type: Outcrops in woods
Land status: Pine Popple Wild Rivers (State of Wisconsin)
Material: Red tourmaline
Host rock: Early Proterozoic quartz-mica gneiss
Difficulty: Hard
Family-friendly: No, hiking is short but intense
Tools needed: None, Wild Rivers Property
Special concerns: Outcrop can be hard to find
Special attractions: Fishing in Pine River
GPS parking: N45° 51.233' / W88° 20.983'
GPS "trail" entrance: N45° 51.200' / W88° 21.183'
GPS pegmatite outcrop: N45° 51.033' / W88° 21.117'

This part of the outcrop has a vein with purple minerals and it is in extremely hard rock.

Topographic quadrangle: Florence SE, WI
Finding the site: Take WI 101 to where it crosses the Pine River. East of the river is a canoe access point and parking. Park at this area, and walk across the bridge (west) and look for the best place to start walking south into the woods on the south side of SR 101. There is no trail that leads to the site. The entrance to the best way to walk into the woods is marked with some boulders along the road, but these boulders are only meant to keep vehicles out and do not mark a trailhead.

Rockhounding

The Animikie Red Ace pegmatite in Florence County, Wisconsin is a good example of a site that is well worth visiting, even though collecting is not allowed. This site has red tourmaline, known as rubellite, and it is relatively easy to access, although the hike can be challenging. This site is located west of the Pine River and south of SR 101 near the Wisconsin–Michigan border.

The tourmaline crystals are distinct but they grew deep within the quartz and not exposed in vugs or other pockets.

Tourmaline is a complex cyclosilicate found in granitic pegmatites, and occurs as an accessory mineral in igneous and metamorphic rocks. Black tourmaline, known as schorl, is common in granitic and gneissic rocks that crystallized at relatively high temperatures. Although common, black tourmaline is still an interesting mineral to collect, as it often forms radiating and distinct elongated crystals.

Colored tourmalines are among the most prized gemstones. The color of tourmaline can vary greatly and it depends on the composition of the surrounding rock. Black tourmaline is iron-bearing, and due to the abundance of iron in most rocks it is not surprising that it is the most common variety of tourmaline. Brown tourmaline, known as dravite, is magnesium-bearing and is also relatively common.

Lithium-bearing tourmalines are generally light colored and can have a variety of different shades. Elbaite is a gem variety of tourmaline and often forms long multicolored semitransparent prisms, which include shades of green (verdelite), blue (indicolite), and pink to red (rubellite). Elbaite tourmalines are among the most prized tourmalines, and get their name from the island of Elba off the west coast of Italy.

Rubellite tourmaline gets its name from the Latin word *rubellus*, which means red. While rubellite tourmalines are found in lithium-rich rocks, it is manganese that gives rubellite its red color. However, the presence of manganese often results in more inclusions in the mineral, and this reduces the quality of the gemstone. Clear, deep red rubellite tourmaline is very rare and is among the most valuable of the colored tourmalines.

The rubellite tourmaline deposit in Florence County is relatively well-documented in the geologic literature. The tourmaline occurs in the Animikie Red Ace pegmatite. The pegmatite is found in a large outcrop of Precambrian gneiss on the east side of a hill above Pine Creek. The outcrop has some small drill holes, indicating that someone was either getting ready to blast, or perhaps simply removing cores for academic research. There were several broken rocks around the deposit, evidence that others were here to look for tourmaline.

The exposed rocks have several bands of tourmaline mineralization in place that obviously could not be easily broken out. Nature has a way of protecting outcrops from collectors, and there is nothing that protects an outcrop like a smooth, flush face of solid granite. These bands are one of the prime attractions for mineralogists at the site. Unfortunately, since this area is within the Pine-Popples Wild Rivers area, collecting is not allowed, but you can take as many photographs as you would like with your camera.

References: Cordua, 1998; Beard, 2010; Sirbescu et al., 2008

56. Florence Iron Mine

County: Florence
Site type: Former Iron Mine
Land status: Uncertain, not posted
Material: Hematite and limonite
Host rock: Proterozoic Riverton Iron Formation
Difficulty: Moderate
Family-friendly: No
Tools needed: Hammer
Special concerns: Mine highwalls are extremely steep, difficult hike to mine
Special attractions: Iron Mountain Iron Mine Tour in Michigan
GPS parking: N45º 55.550' / W88º 15.717'
GPS eastern end of mine: N45º 55.583' / W88º 15.617'
Topographic quadrangle: Florence West, WI-MI
Finding the site: From the intersection of WI 70 and US 141 on the west side of Florence, go west on US 141 for 0.3 mile. Look for a substation on your right. Park at the rear of the substation, away from the access roads that may be used for the station, and hike southeast to an indistinct road that goes past the east end of the mine. From here hike into the long narrow pit formed by the mine. It is highly recommended to navigate your way to the mine with a smartphone and satellite photo as the footpaths are indistinct.

Rockhounding

This is a former iron mine just west of Florence that I assume is the Florence mine. The mine is a narrow open cut that mined the Riverton Iron Formation in the Wisconsin section of the Menominee iron range. Iron ore was first discovered near Florence in 1873, and the Florence Mine was one of the first mines developed. Ore was not shipped until 1880, and the mine continued to produce until 1931. Total shipments of ore from the Florence Mine were estimated to be 3,700,000 tons. Much of the mining was reported to be underground. Most of the ore was of relatively low quality and the Florence Mine, as well most of the mines in the area, were all closed for good by the early 1960s.

The mine extracted iron ore from the Middle Precambrian Riverton Iron Formation, which is part of the Paint River Group. The Paint River Group is mainly clastic sediments, such as sand and mud, interlayered with chert.

The sides of the former iron mine are sheer cliffs.

The Riverton Iron Formation contains iron–rich minerals including siderite, hematite, limonite, magnetite, and grunerite with interlayered chert.

I visited this mine in 2012 and 2016. During my first visit I parked at the substation and was able to hike to the eastern end of the pit. It was a terrible

Lots of mineralized rock is present on the sides of the mine but the rocks are difficult and dangerous to reach.

climb over fallen trees and through briars, but I was able to force a path to the mine. The sides of the mine pit are extremely steep, and the bottom of the mine pit is a deep narrow lake. On the south side near the waterline I could see evidence of former underground workings. The sides of the mine are full of iron-rich rocks, and many of these are much more colorful than typical iron mines in the region. I found an abundance of yellow, orange, and red rocks. The yellow and orange were limonite, and the red was hematite. I did not see any indications of siderite and all the minerals appeared to be oxidized, and I did not see any magnetite or grunerite in the mine.

This was a difficult site to reach. When I returned in 2016 I tried to hike the same way into the pit, and I was with my son and daughter, who were 22 and 20 respectively, so they could handle a moderate hike. We tried to enter the mine from the eastside but were blocked by the fallen trees and briars. We returned to the car, and by then they had had enough. They decided to stay in the car, and I attempted to reach the mine by the west side. There is a powerline easement along the west side so it was a relatively easy but steep hike.

The colors of the rocks in the mine include yellow and red from limonite and hematite and silver from the specular hematite.

I came across some small dumps of iron-rich shaly rocks, along with a snake, but these rocks were not as colorful as the rocks in the east end of the mine. I soon bushwhacked my way through the woods along some deer trails and came to the western end of the mine. Unfortunately, the highwalls here are sheer and extremely dangerous. You can easily lose your footing and plummet 60 feet into the icy cold water of the mine, and you would likely hit some tree branches on the way down for good measure. I realized at that point that I was pushing too hard to get to the mine, and I immediately began backing away from the edge of the pit. This area is very deceptive, and what appears to be good footing may be slippery or an area with no underlying support. I highly recommend sticking to the eastern end of the mine, as this can be approached in a safer manner.

References: Dutton, 1971; Johnson, 1958; Sims, 1992; USGS, 2004

57. Mountain Precambrian Feldspar

The outcrops on the west side of Hwy. 32 have best crystals of feldspar.

County: Oconto
Site type: Roadcut
Land status: Nicolet National Forest, highway right-of-way
Material: Feldspar crystals in gneiss
Host rock: Middle Proterozoic metasediments and metavolcanics
Difficulty: Easy
Family-friendly: Yes
Tools needed: Hammer
Special concerns: Traffic on WI 32
Special attractions: Bass Lake Recreation Area
GPS parking: N45° 14.800' / W88° 30.883'

Miarolitic cavities in the gneiss and granite often contain crystals of potassium feldspar.

Topographic quadrangle: Shadow Lake, WI
Finding the site: From the intersection of WI 64 and WI 32, take WI 32 north for 2.9 miles. Turn right onto Donnelly Lane and park on the shoulder of Donnelly Lane. The gneiss with the feldspar crystals is on the opposite (west) side of WI 32.

Rockhounding

Any time you see an outcrop in northern Wisconsin it is often worth checking out. Outcrops tend to be rare in these regions that are covered with glacial till. These outcrops differ from many of other bedrock outcrops in the region as they are gneissic rocks as opposed to the more common granite that you often seen in the region.

The gneisses are broken up on the slope of the roadcut and it is easy to find unweathered pieces. I found several pieces that had vugs with small but distinct orange feldspar crystals. Breaking these rocks apart sometimes revealed additional vugs. I also found several pieces with dark red feldspar, and

Many of the larger pieces of orange feldspar show excellent cleavage and reflect well in the sunlight.

several pieces with long, wide orange feldspar crystals. Some of the cleavage planes for the feldspars were more than two inches long, and they reflected well in the sunlight.

References: Cordua, 1998; Sims et al., 1991

SITES 57 & 58

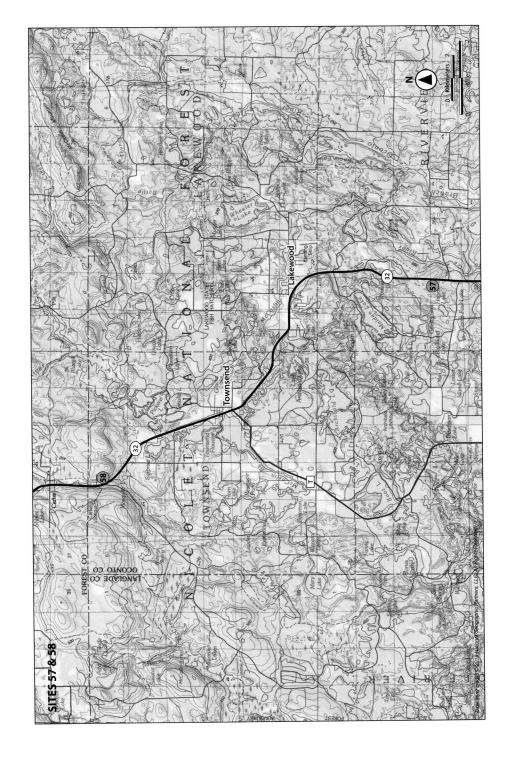

58. Quartz Hill Precambrian Quartz Crystals

These are some of the quartz crystals found on the ground surface.

County: Oconto
Site type: Outcrops on mountainside
Land status: Nicolet National Forest
Material: Quartz crystals
Host rock: Early Proterozoic quartzite of the Pembine-Wausau terrane
Difficulty: Easy
Family-friendly: Yes
Tools needed: Hammer
Special concerns: Sharp rocks, moderate hike to site
Special attractions: Cathedral Pines State Natural Area
GPS parking: N45º 22.483' / W88º 37.733'
GPS quartz crystals: N45º 22.383' / W88º 37.367'

Topographic quadrangle: Townsend, WI
Finding the site: From the intersection of WI 64 and WI 32, take WI 32 north for 14.9 miles. Turn left (west) onto Carter Tower Road, and park here. The trail to Quartz Hill is on the east side of the highway. It has a boardwalk to cross the swampy area and then continues about 0.3 mile to the quartz crystal site.

Rockhounding

This is a classic locality for quartz crystals in the region. It is easy to find and there is plenty of space for parking. The outcrops are reached by crossing the road and following a short section on a boardwalk and then up the trail for about 0.3 mile to the site. Quartz Hill is the western extension of McCaslin Mountain, which is a large mountain of Early Proterozoic quartzite that lies to the east. The quartzite is maroon but locally white, gray, and red. Quartz crystals can be found loose in the soil, in loose rocks around the mountain, and in small voids in the host rock. Digging for crystals is prohibited by the Forest Service, but you are still allowed to collect small amounts of the crystals from the surface.

This is the west side of Quartz Hill, and quartz crystals can be found in veins and loose rocks of this area.

The best place to find loose quartz crystals is in the ground just north of the main part of quartz hill. A sign lets you know you are at Quartz Hill, and there is also a sign that says "No Digging for Quartz Allowed." Quartz crystals can be found just upslope from this area. The crystals include those with terminated points and penetrations. The best way to find them is to watch the ground for the reflection off the crystal faces, and you can also sift through the dirt by hand. Digging with tools, such as a shovel, is prohibited.

There are several large rocks in this area that have quartz crystals, and the main mass of Quartz Hill has several zones with vein quartz and crystals. The slope on the west side of Quartz Hill has several large boulders and rocks and quartz crystals can also be found in this area. The quartz can be quite sharp, and if you break any pieces with your hammer, be careful of flying quartz. In 2008 I was at the site and later found out that my lower leg was lacerated by sharp quartz. My sock was soaked with blood and I did not even notice it until I took off my boot. Our Chihuahua promptly tried to eat my sock.

I highly recommend safety glasses, gloves, steel-toed boots, and long pants at this site, along with lots of insect repellent. Although digging for quartz is prohibited you will certainly be able to find crystals on the surface and within the rocks.

References: Beard, 2002; Cordua, 1998; Sims et al., 1991

59. Irma Hill Cambrian Sandstone

The site is just north of CR-J, but the only safe parking is about 2,000 feet west of the roadcut.

County: Lincoln
Site type: Hillside/Roadcut Outcrops
Land status: Uncertain, not posted
Material: Sandstone
Host rock: Cambrian Sandstone
Difficulty: Easy
Family-friendly: Yes
Tools needed: Hammer
Special concerns: Traffic along CR-J
Special attractions: None
GPS parking: N45° 21.100' / W89° 39.917'
GPS outcrops: N45° 21.100' / W89° 39.433'
Topographic quadrangle: Irma, WI

Many of the rocks have white interiors of nearly pure quartz.

Finding the site: From WI 52 in Wausau, take US 51 28.4 miles north to Irma. Turn right (east) onto CR-J. Park at the first wide turnout on the right (south) side of CR-J. This was safest place to park that I could find on this road near the outcrops. From the parking area walk approximately 2,000 feet east, and the outcrops will be on the left (north) side of the road.

Rockhounding

Nearly all of Lincoln County is covered by Pleistocene glacial sediments, and this obscures nearly all the Precambrian bedrock. Rocks are further covered by dense forests and farmland, and outcrops and roadcuts are limited due to relatively low relief. The bedrock is known to be primarily Precambrian metavolcanic rocks, but there are some limited exposure of early Paleozoic rocks in the area.

Irma Hill, located just east of Irma on CR-J, has outcrops of what is believed to be Cambrian sandstone. The sandstone was deposited long after Proterozoic quartzite on Rib Mountain, which is to the south. However, due to the limited exposures, the stratigraphic relationship between the sandstone

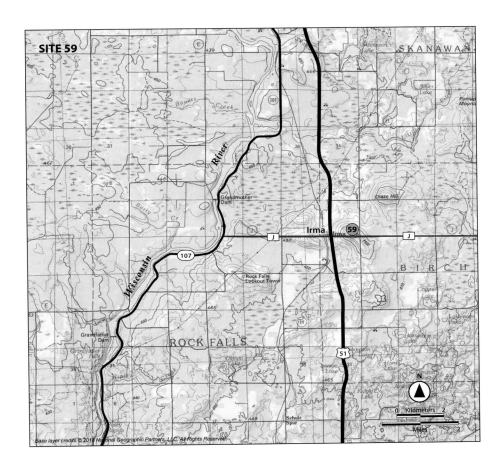

on Irma Hill and other early Paleozoic sediments in northern Wisconsin is not clear.

The outcrops at Irma Hill reportedly have soft-bodied fossils and ripple marks, and I explored the site to find these features. CR-J did not have many places for parking so I parked about 2,000 feet west of the outcrops at a safe place to park my vehicle. I then walked to the outcrops. The outcrops are numerous and consist of nearly horizontal beds of hard, well-cemented sandstone. The sandstone is white on freshly broken surfaces but the exterior of the rocks is generally stained a light orange.

I was not able to find any fossils or ripple marks, and while this was disappointing, I was intrigued by the coarse rounded sand grains that make up the rock. The rock is well cemented and extremely hard. Unlike sandstones that also have abundant feldspar and dark minerals, this sandstone is nearly entirely quartz. I have not seen many sandstones with such a high degree of roundness and purity. If not for the slight iron staining the hill would likely be bright white.

This sandstone is tightly cemented and would be difficult to crush, but the grains are rounded and if crushed would likely make a good sand for hydraulic fracturing of oil and natural gas wells. However, given the limited extent of the sandstone at Irma Hill, and the fact that the hill is already occupied by a radio tower, the sandstone will not be quarried at any time in the foreseeable future.

References: Dott and Attig, 2004, Bostwick and Hess, 2015

60. Little Chicago Precambrian Metabasalt

The actinolite is fine grained and compact as the parent rock is a greenstone.

County: Marathon
Site type: Roadcut
Land status: Highway right-of-way, not posted
Material: Fine-grained actinolite and metabasalt
Host rock: Precambrian Metabasalt
Difficulty: Easy
Family-friendly: No, not much space on roadside
Tools needed: Hammer
Special concerns: Traffic can be heavy
Special attractions: Rib Falls
GPS parking/roadcut: N45° 02.817' / W89° 47.40'
Topographic quadrangle: Little Chicago, WI

Finding the site: From WI 29, take exit 156 for WI 107 and head north for 7.1 miles to Little Chicago. At Little Chicago, turn right (east) onto CR-A, and continue east for 2.7 miles to the roadcut, which is on the first hill east of the Little Rib River. Parking is best on the north side of CR-A, so you may have to make a U-turn to position your vehicle on the north side.

Rockhounding

I first learned of references to "jade" in Wisconsin in the early 2000s. Jade is a fine-grained translucent rock that composed of the pyroxene jadeite or an amphibole in the tremolite-ferroactinolite series, which is referred to as nephrite jade. A *Lapidary Journal* article by Wilson (1958) on Mindat.com indicated that jade occurred near the Little Rib River in Marathon County. I was immediately skeptical but had to check it out. A review of maps indicated that the Little Rib River crossed CR-A approximately 2.5 miles east of Little Chicago.

I first visited the area in 2001. The area around the Little Rib River was private land, so I went looking for roadcuts where the basement rocks would be exposed. Driving east on CR-A, I found a large roadcut of fine-grained dark green rocks east of the Little Rib River. The roadcut exposed the dark green rocks on both sides of CR-A. Unfortunately during my first visit it was pouring rain, and it was difficult to explore the roadcut.

In addition to the deposit described by Wilson in 1958, two prospectors found a nephrite outcrop in the Rib River area in 1958. Unfortunately the Rib River drainage has two principal branches, the Big Rib and the Little Rib Rivers. A locality described as the Rib River area was not specific enough to find this outcrop.

I later visited the roadcut on CR-A several more times when in the Marathon area, and got to observe the outcrop in detail. Many of the other bedrock exposures in the region are weathered granitic and gneissic rocks, and this was one of the few mafic exposures I have seen in the region. The rock is dark green and fine-grained, and the main mineral appears to be actinolite. The outcrop has some zones of slickensides and some light green to gray bands. The rock is also extremely hard. It was difficult to break any pieces off the outcrop, and the loose rocks at the base were also extremely hard. I was not able to confirm if this material contained any nephrite, but it is dark green, fine-grained, extremely hard, and composed of what appears to be a compact dark green actinolite. I cannot confirm if the rock is jade, so I have described this site as an actinolite locality.

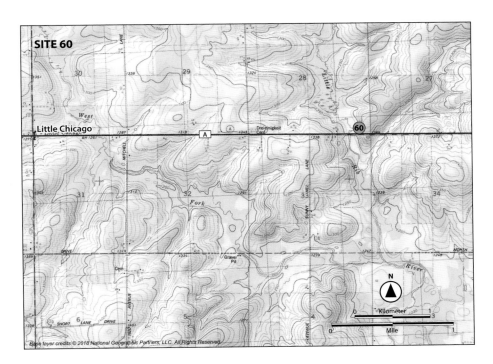

I later found out that in 2015 a company known as Wisconsin Jade was marketing material from another nephrite deposit in northern Marathon County. This rock was reportedly verified as a fine-grained tremolite-ferroactinolite, which qualifies it as nephrite jade. The material was also endorsed by the Gemological Institute of America in 2014 as nephrite jade. The rock has been described as a highly brecciated mafic to ultramafic rock that was replaced by tremolite-ferroactinolite.

I reviewed the Google Maps satellite photos for the area, and I did not see any indications of recent workings in the Little Rib River area. Even if I could locate the workings by recent satellite photos, it would likely be difficult to get access to the deposits. For now I am going to have to settle for the dark green material in the roadcut.

References: Wilson, 1958; Cordua, 2017

61. Stettin Precambrian Moonstone

Hints of rainbow schiller can be seen when tilting these feldspars in the sunlight.

County: Marathon
Site type: Roadcut
Land status: Highway right-of-way, not posted
Material: Weathered coarse-grained pyroxene syenite
Host rock: Syenite
Difficulty: Easy
Family-friendly: Yes
Tools needed: Hammer
Special concerns: Traffic
Special attractions: Rib Mountain State Park
GPS parking/roadcut: N44° 59.283' / W89° 44.900'
Topographic quadrangle: Wausau West, WI

The feldspars are exposed in this small roadcut on the north side of CR-U.

Finding the site: From WI 29, take exit 156 for WI 107 and head north for 2.9 miles to the intersection with CR-U. Turn right (east) on U, and proceed 4.5 miles to a small exposure of rock on the north side of CR-U. Make a U-turn and park on the north side of the road so you do not have to cross the road. The moonstone can be found among the rocks in this exposure.

Rockhounding

I had heard many stories about moonstone in Marathon County, but I never had much information about the exact locality. The information that I had was not very specific. The moonstone outcrops were reported to be on CR-U, and east of the Little Rib River, and within the Stettin Pluton. CR-U is a long east west trending road and this did not narrow down the area.

The Stettin pluton is oldest and most alkaline pluton in the Wausau intrusive complex. The pluton is Middle Proterozoic in age and has been dated as 1.570 billion years old. Much of the pluton is a syenite and contains zones of pyroxene syenite, amphibole syenite, tabular syenite, and nepheline syenite. It is located northwest of Wausau and comprises a low hilly area. The pluton

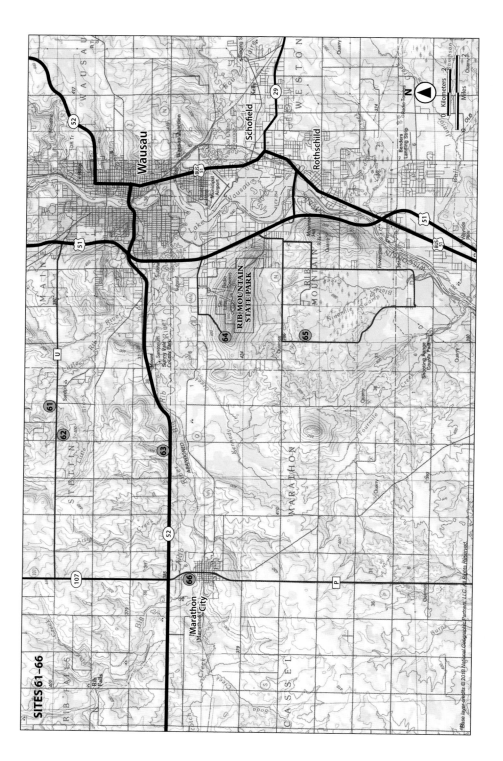

SITES 61–66

This large piece was found on the ground right outside of our vehicle.

is poorly exposed and is covered by swamps, forests, and farmlands. The only accessible exposures are in roadcuts and some of the larger rivers and streams, and these are hard to find due to the low relief of the area.

After much research, I finally found a reference (Myers et al., 1984) that described a roadcut with "moonstone" dikes in a pyroxene–amphibole syenite. Most importantly, the area was shown on a topographic map. My wife and I stopped at the site in September 2017. The roadcut had intrusive rocks exposed, and I was able to find some small pieces of feldspar with a tiny bit of schiller, which is the colorful iridescence seen in moonstone. My wife found a large piece of this feldspar right outside of our car. Just west of these exposures I found an area that had been dug in the hillside next to the road. This also had several small pieces of broken feldspar with minor schiller. Other rockhounds had also been digging at this site, which was also a sign that I had finally come to the right place for the moonstone.

References: Myers et al. 1984; Falster, 1986

62. Stettin Precambrian Feldspar

County: Marathon
Site type: Roadcut
Land status: Highway right-of-way, not posted
Material: Weathered coarse-grained potassium feldspar
Host rock: Granite
Difficulty: Easy
Family-friendly: Yes
Tools needed: Hammer
Special concerns: Land status uncertain
Special attractions: Rib River Park north of Marathon City
GPS parking/roadcut: N45° 02.817' / W89° 47.400'
Topographic quadrangle: Marathon, WI
Finding the site: From WI 29, take exit 156 for WI 107 and head north for 2.9 miles to the intersection with CR-U. Turn right (east) on U, and proceed 3.1 miles to the intersection of CR-O. Cross the intersection and pull over on the shoulder. The feldspar is loose on the ground on the south side of CR-O.

Rockhounding

I originally came to this site in search of moonstone, which was reported on CR-U. During one of my many trips to the area I noticed an elevated section on the south side of CR-U just east of CR-O. Most importantly, there was an area here to safely pull over. The road at this area is full of weathered potassium feldspar, and much of this was a light tan to orange. The rocks had a granitic texture and minor quartz was present, indicating that this was likely a quartz syenite or granite as opposed to a quartz-free syenite.

I was able to find some nice small pieces of potassium feldspar, which I often referred to as K-feldspar. Breaking these apart with my hammer revealed unweathered sections with good cleavage. The area next to the road was not posted, and I walked southward to a group of trees and briars. The ground sloped to a drainage and I hoped to find some ground where bedrock was better exposed. I soon found some loose rocks on the ground and then a large pile of broken rocks that were nearly all fine to coarse-grained granite/quartz syenite with large feldspar crystals. This pile was obscured by briars, and my arms and legs were cut by the thorns. Fortunately I had a pair of gloves to protect my hands. This was in early July and the vegetation

This rock was found on the surface at the site and has several large intergrown feldspar crystals.

was thick. I found several pieces with large K-feldspars, and closer inspection revealed small sections of quartz-feldspar intergrowths resembling graphic granite. Some of the K-feldspars were almost two inches long and the crystal outline was clearly defined in the rock.

I later broke apart many of the coarse-grained rocks and split the individual feldspar crystals. I was looking for signs of color and opalescent luster indicative of moonstone but did not find any. While I did not find any moonstone, this site offer some good pieces of K-feldspar with good cleavage, and it is worth a stop if you are traveling along CR-U or CR-O in the area.

References: Sims, 1992; Sood et al., 1980; Falster, 1986

63. Wausau Precambrian Gneisses and Granites

County: Marathon
Site type: Roadcut
Land status: Highway right-of-way, not posted
Material: Gneissic and granitic rocks
Host rock: Foliated rocks of Wausau Syenite Complex
Difficulty: Easy
Family-friendly: Yes
Tools needed: Hammer
Special concerns: Land status uncertain
Special attractions: Rib Mountain State Park
GPS parking/roadcut: N44° 56.833' / W89° 46.467'
Topographic quadrangle: Marathon, WI
Finding the site: From WI 29, take the exit to CR-O, which is the exit between exits 147 and 152. This is a brand new exit and at the time of this writing it did not have a number. I anticipate it will be exit 149 or 50, based on mileage from the other exits along WI 29. When you take the exit, turn north on CR-O, and you will be able to see the roadcuts. The cuts are especially prominent at the intersection of CR-O and the appropriately named Rock Cut Road, which used to be North 120th Ave. When I approached the area I came south on CR-O, and parked at an accessible space on the side of the road, which is just east of the exposed outcrops.

Rockhounding

I first noticed this site when driving south on CR-O to WI 29 with my family. As we approached WI 29 I noticed that the flat terrain had yielded to bedrock exposures. At this point my family had had enough rock collecting for the day, so I was not able to stop. However, a few days later I was able to stop for a good look and walk along the exposures.

The rocks at these roadcuts are part of the Wausau Syenite Complex. This is part of a northeast–southwest trending belt of anorogenic granite plutons that extend from the Scandinavia to the southwest United States. Anorogenic plutons are crustal magmas that crystallized in a tectonic setting unrelated to collision of lithospheric plates and formation of mountain belts. This differs from orogenic magmas that formed along subduction zones where oceanic

This roadcut in Precambrian rocks covers a long stretch of road.

and continental plates collide, such as the granitic rocks that form the Sierra Nevada Mountains of California. The Wausau Syenite Complex formed at about the same time as the nearby Wolf River Batholith, and these rocks formed approximately 1.5 billion years ago.

Since outcrops are so hard to find in central Wisconsin I thought this would be a good place to see freshly exposed rocks. A review on Google Maps indicated that this was a relatively new roadcut. I parked at a small turnout on the north side of CR-O close to where this north–south road turned to the west, and this was near the eastern end of the roadcut. This was in early July and the grass was thick along the base of the exposures.

The rocks are mix of granitic and metamorphic rocks. Geologic maps indicate that this is an area of calc-alkaline intrusive rocks that include granite, granodiorite, tonalite and quartz diorite, and my field observations indicate there is also an abundance of fine-grained dark rocks that resemble metabasalt. The rocks range from fine-grained to coarse -grained and are often coarsely foliated. The dominant minerals are feldspar, quartz, and pyroxenes, but I did not see any zones of quartz crystals, feldspar phenocrysts, or other areas of

This fine-grained mafic dike cut across this felsic intrusive rock, and these types of rocks are seen throughout the roadcut.

unusual mineralization. This area appears to be highly metamorphosed intrusive and metamorphic rocks that formed at the same time as the larger granitic and syenitic plutons of the Wausau Syenite Complex. While the outcrops lack any unusual mineralization, they are still worth a visit as this is the largest fresh exposure I seen in the Northern Highland of Wisconsin.

References: LaBerge and Myers, 1972; Myers et al., 1984

64. Rib Mountain Precambrian Quartzite

This was a large quarry that was operated by 3M in early to mid-twentieth century.

County: Marathon
Site type: Former Quarry
Land status: Rib Mountain State Park
Material: Quartzite
Host rock: Early Proterozoic Quartzite
Difficulty: Easy
Family-friendly: Yes
Tools needed: None, no collecting (State Park)
Special concerns: Can get hot in summer, be sure to bring water
Special attractions: Rib Mountain State Park
GPS parking: N44° 55.767' / W89° 41.750'
GPS quarry: N44° 55.417' / W89° 42.533'

The quartzite is nearly pure quartz and bright white in the sunlight.

Topographic quadrangle: Wausau West, WI
Finding the site: From US 51 on the west side of Wausau, take exit 190 to North Mountain Road/CR-NN. Continue 1.5 miles west, and turn left (south) onto Grouse Lane. Follow this 0.3 mile to the trailhead. Parking may be limited so you may have to park far from the trailhead. From the end of the road at the trailhead, take the Turkey Vulture Trail, and stay to the right. Hike approximately 0.8 mile, and you will see the entrance to the former quarry to your left (south).

Rockhounding

Rib Mountain is a prominent monadnock of Early Proterozoic quartzite. A monadnock is an isolated hill or ridge that rises above the surrounding eroded plain. It is an erosional remnant as it was much more resistant to erosion than the surrounding rocks.

The quartzite was first mined in 1893 to manufacture sandpaper. The Wausau Sandpaper Company was incorporated in 1900 and built a factory, and the Wausau Quartz Company crushed the quartzite for grinding and polishing purposes. The companies merged into Wausau Abrasives, and

The quarry floor gets wet and muddy when it rains, but fortunately during our visit it was very dry.

Minnesota Mining and Manufacturing (3M) bought the companies in 1929. The new company under 3M reportedly operated until the 1990s, but I suspect operations at the quarry ended well before then. I could not find documentation that they operated the quarry into the 1990s, and this seems unlikely due to the lack of equipment and a paved road to the mine.

The site is reached by a relatively short (0.8 mile) uphill hike on the Turkey Vulture Trail to the quarry. The quarry floor is flat and the highwalls are steep. The rocks are almost entirely quartz and very little iron staining is present. The rocks throughout the quarry are relatively uniform and all parts of the quarry offer good places to see pure quartzite. Be sure to bring water and sunglasses, as it gets hot in the quarry and the sun reflects strongly against the white quartzite.

References: Lackey et al., 2009

65. Rib Mountain Rotten Granite

County: Marathon
Site type: Roadside rocks
Land status: Likely road right-of-way, not posted
Material: Reddish-Orange Rotten Granite
Host rock: Precambrian Granite
Difficulty: Easy
Family-friendly: Yes
Tools needed: Hammer
Special concerns: Land status uncertain
Special attractions: Rib Mountain State Park
GPS parking: N44° 53.567' / W89° 42.650'
Topographic quadrangle: Wausau West, WI
Finding the site: From US 51, take exit 188 to Rib Mountain Drive, and continue southwest for about 0.1 mile. Turn left (south) onto South Mountain Road, and continue on this road for 3.2 miles. Turn left (south) onto Red Bud Road, and go 0.6 mile. Turn left (east) onto Blackberry Road. The site is at the northeast corner of the intersection of Red Bud Road and Blackberry Road.

Rockhounding

Rotten granite is granite that has weathered or otherwise altered to the point where it crumbles. This is often the result of the feldspars converting to clay minerals and biotite converting to chlorite. The resulting rock is often used for athletic field surfaces, such as baseball diamonds and for pathways and other surfaces. The rotten granite can be easily sized and is durable. It also provides good drainage.

The granite quarries in Marathon County are well known for their rotten granite. Unfortunately, they are on private land and difficult to access on short notice. This site, which is adjacent to rotten granite quarries, has some granite boulders along the roadside and some rotten granite on the surface.

Rotten granite is also known for smoky quartz and feldspar crystals. Many years ago I had the opportunity to collect in the quarry that is just north of this site. I was able to find some smoky quartz and vugs with feldspar crystals. Unfortunately, that site has since been posted against trespassing.

Rotten granite is present at this site along the roadside. The granite boulders are relatively intact but you can find both hand–sized granite pieces

The granite on the ground can be described as "rotten" but there are several unweathered granitic boulders at the site.

and lots of small, popcorn-size pieces of rotten granite. I did not find any quartz or vugs with feldspar crystals but was still pleased by another first-hand look at the rotten granite

References: Cordua, 1998; USGS, 2004

66. Marathon Big Rib River Park Granite

The granite is in a drainage just north of the road next to the parking area.

County: Marathon
Site type: Drainage Ditch
Land status: City Park
Material: Reddish-Orange Granite
Host rock: Precambrian Granite
Difficulty: Easy
Family-friendly: Yes
Tools needed: Hammer
Special concerns: Collecting likely not allowed in City Park
Special attractions: Fishing in Big Rib River
GPS parking: N44º 56.124' / W89º 50.548'
Topographic quadrangle: Marathon, WI

The granite was brought to the area for drainage control and is a good representation of what is in the local quarries.

Finding the site: From WI 29, take exit 156 to WI 107 south. Go 0.4 mile and turn left (east) on Krautkramer Lane. In 350 feet, turn left (north) onto River Road. Follow this about 0.2 mile into the park. Park at the parking area, and walk over to a small drainage just west of the parking area. The granite is in loose pieces in the drainage.

Rockhounding

This is an unusual locality as the granite at this location was brought to this drainage area for construction. The granite is a distinct reddish-orange and is coarse-grained. It almost certainly came from one of the local quarries. Unfortunately all the local quarries are on private ground and it can be difficult to get access. This site has granite that is likely similar to the granite found in many of the quarries.

67. Jim Falls Gneiss and Granite

The gneiss is best exposed when river levels are low.

County: Chippewa
Site type: River bank outcrops and loose rocks
Land status: Uncertain, but has public access
Material: Banded gneiss and granite
Host rock: Precambrian gneiss and granite
Difficulty: Easy
Family-friendly: Yes
Tools needed: None
Special concerns: Slippery rocks near river
Special attractions: None
GPS parking-bridge: N45° 03.317' / W91° 16.450'
GPS parking-wayside park: N45° 03.517' / W91° 16.267'
GPS outcrops in river: N45° 03.283' / W91° 16.433'
Topographic quadrangle: Jim Falls, WI
Finding the site: This is a locality with two stops. I recommend stopping first at the parking area at the bridge and then hiking down the short trail to the river.

The gneiss has areas of migmatites and is highly polished by the river.

To get to the bridge parking area, take WI 29 to exit 79, and go north on WI 178, which is also known as Seymour Cray Sr. Boulevard. Continue north on WI 178 for 13.8 miles. Park at the small turnout before the bridge that crosses the Chippewa River. This bridge is closed to traffic. Do not turn onto County Trunk Y bridge, as this is an active bridge, and it is just south of the parking area. From the closed bridge you can hike to the river bed.

To get to the second site, simply proceed 0.3 mile north of the first parking area, and pull in at the wayside park that has a historical marker to "Old Abe," a bald eagle that was a mascot of the 8th Wisconsin Volunteer Infantry in the Civil War. Park here, and walk toward the river. The rocks at this site are loose boulders and large rocks of granite and gneiss that were placed just north of the trail and in the woods.

Rockhounding

This is an excellent site to see banded Precambrian amphibolites and hornblende gneiss with granitic dikes and small pegmatites. These are some of the oldest rocks in the area and are mapped as Late Archean Gneiss, migmatite, and amphibolite. They are about 2.8 billion years old, which is older than many of the granite intrusions in Wisconsin.

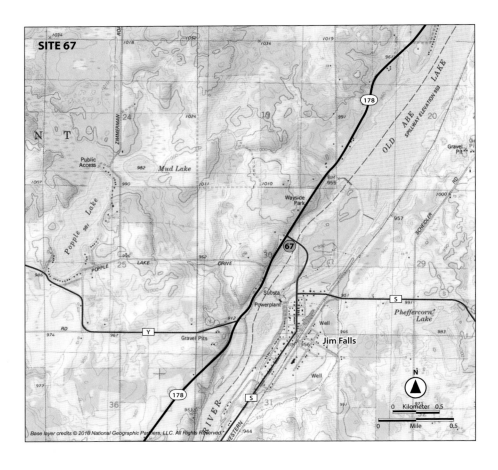

Some of the best exposures of the gneiss are in the Chippewa River near the bridge at the first parking area, which is south of the upper dam of the Jim Falls area. The gneisses have been polished by the Chippewa River and are best exposed during times of low water. The area is quite scenic, and during our visit to the site we saw a photographer with a large amount of camera equipment taking photographs of the river near the bridge. Most of the smaller pieces of banded gneiss are in the river and hard to access, so it is difficult to find good hand-sample sized pieces of the gneiss, at least in the outcrops near the bridge.

At the second locality the rocks are not at the river but in the woods just north of the trail. There is a large pile of loose granite and gneiss that appears

Loose granitic boulders with coarse feldspar are present between the wayside park and the river.

to have been placed there many years ago. This may have been to control erosion or for some other project related to the dam sites. Many of the rocks here are coarse-grained granites that have abundant orange feldspar. While these do not appear to be from the rocks in the river, they are still worth exploring for coarse feldspar and related minerals.

References: Barrett, 1865; Myers et al., 1974; Cordua, 1998

68. Powell Precambrian Kyanite

The kyanite schist is well foliated and the blue kyanite roughly parallels the foliation.

County: Iron
Site type: Outcrop on roadside
Land status: Northern Highland American Legion State Forest
Material: Kyanite in biotite schist
Host rock: Early Proterozoic biotite schist
Difficulty: Easy
Family-friendly: Yes
Tools needed: Hammer
Special concerns: Must park well off highway
Special attractions: None
GPS parking: N46° 04.950' / W90° 00.283'
Topographic quadrangle: Wilson Lake, WI
Finding the site: From Powell, take WI 47 approximately 1.0 miles to where it intersects WI 182. Turn left on WI 182, and head west. Go 1.2 miles and look

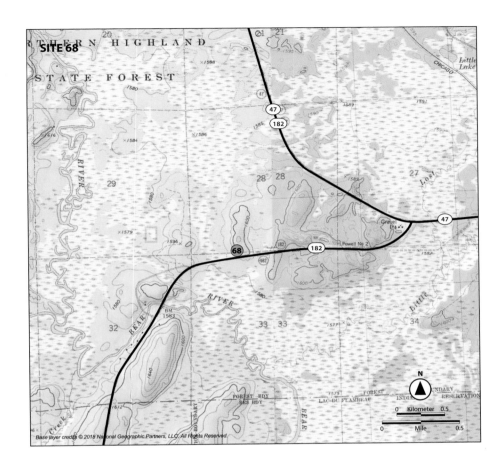

for a small outcrop on the north side of WI 182. Parking is adequate along the
north side of the highway, but be sure to pull off as far as possible. WI 182 gets a
surprising amount of traffic.

Rockhounding

This is a small but worthwhile outcrop to explore for kyanite crystals in biotite schist. The area is heavily wooded and exposures are not common, and
this is the only outcrop that I saw in the area. While this limits your area for
collecting, it certainly makes it easy to know that you are at the right outcrop.
This outcrop is apparently well known to other rockhounds and visitors to
the area. The outcrop had at least four small piles of rocks that resemble cairns,
and the rocks showed indications of hammering.

The kyanite is light gray to blue, and occurs as short, stubby crystals as opposed to the long bladed kyanite crystals found in many kyanite mines. The kyanite is found in a coarse, well-foliated Early Proterozoic biotite schist. The main outcrop is hard and smooth, and some of the better pieces of kyanite can be found by going into the woods and looking for exposed rocks. The rocks are well foliated and while the host rock can be described as a schist, some of the rocks are much coarser grained and are better described as biotite gneiss.

Garnet is common at this locality, and staurolite is also reported. During my visit to the site I also went looking for other outcrops nearby, but did not find any other outcrops. I also took Bridge Road, which is just to the west, and looked for exposures along the Bear River. I did not find any exposures here and later concluded that time at this site is best spent at the outcrop and woods immediately north of the outcrop.

An attempt to mine kyanite in the area was reportedly attempted in the 1930s, but it was not successful. While this is a good locality for rockhounds, it is not hard to see why kyanite mining failed in this area. The kyanite crystals are quite short, and most importantly the kyanite makes up relatively little of the rock. Too much time would be spent separating the kyanite from the biotite, quartz, garnet, and other minerals. Other kyanite deposits outside of Wisconsin provide much better kyanite, and this deposit, like many minor mineral occurrences, never made a long-term viable mine.

References: Cordua, 1998; Sims, 1992; USGS, 2004

69. Montreal Mine Hematite and Magnetite

County: Iron
Site type: Mine dump
Land status: Uncertain, may belong to local government
Material: Hematite and iron formation
Host rock: Early Proterozoic Menominee Group, Ironwood Iron Formation
Difficulty: Easy
Family-friendly: Yes
Tools needed: Hammer
Special concerns: Steep uphill climb on mine dump
Special attractions: None
GPS parking: N46° 25.883' / W90° 13.867'
GPS mine dump: N46° 25.783' / W90° 13.783'
Topographic quadrangle: Ironwood, MI-WI
Finding the site: From the intersection of US 51 and WI 77 in Hurley, take WI 77 west toward Montreal for 2.7 miles. The road soon turns southwest. After you cross the West Fork of the Montreal River, look for a small parking lot to the left (north). Park here and look to the south. You can see the massive mine dump of the former Montreal Mine behind the trees. Cross the road and walk on the ski trail that goes around the east side of the dump near the river. From the trail you then climb to the mine dump.

Rockhounding

The Montreal Mine is a former iron mine that was worked from the late 1800s to the early 1960s. In the mid–1800s the iron-mining industry of Wisconsin was in the southern part of the state. The discovery of large iron deposits in northern Wisconsin in the 1880s shifted the iron-mining industry north, and the southern deposits could not compete with the reserves and easily processed iron ores of northern Wisconsin.

Iron ore was first worked at what became the Montreal mine site in 1882. The mine was named Montreal after the company that worked the ores. The Montreal mine was started as an open pit, but soon became a deep underground mine, with workings nearly 1 mile deep. The Montreal Mine and nearby Cary Mine became among the deepest iron mines in the world.

The rocks on the Montreal Mine dumps are extremely dense and loaded with iron.

However, just as these northern Wisconsin mines put the southern mines out of business, the iron and steel industry soon began to use the large low-grade taconite deposits of the huge open pits mine near Lake Superior in Minnesota. The northern Wisconsin iron mines could not be competitive and the mines soon began to close. The last iron ore was shipped from the Montreal mine in 1962. Today, the massive mine dumps of the Montreal Mine tower over the West Fork of the Montreal River. The dumps can easily be seen from WI 77 as you drive through Montreal.

I first came to Montreal in the summer of 2010 to see if I could get access to any of the former iron mines. Fortunately, I was able to see the mine dumps easily and found parking across the street. The mine dump is next to city hall, and I was able to walk on a trail next to the mine dump. The area was not posted and appeared to be open ground, and I was able to climb up the mine dump and found some interesting pieces of banded iron formation and silvery hematite.

I returned to Montreal in May 2017 to see if the area was still open. I parked in the same place, and the trail I was on was known as the Water

Some of the hematite shows a conchoidal fracture when broken apart.

View Cross-Country Skiing Trail. I was not sure if it was named in 2012, but it appeared that little had changed. I was able to hike up to the dump and I wound up taking the same route I had taken in 2010.

The rocks on the dump are mainly banded iron formation with some red cherty zones and some fine- and coarse-grained hematite. Some of the rocks with hematite are extremely dense. Breaking open some of these rocks exposes the hematite but not all of the rocks have good hematite in their interior. The hematite at this mine is unique in that much of it is silvery-gray and can be found in large masses. This site has ample hematite, and you will be overwhelmed with specimens. You will also soon be reminded that iron ore is extremely heavy and that there are self-imposed limits to what you can collect.

References: Cordua, 1998; Schmidt, 1980; Sims, 1992; USGS, 2004

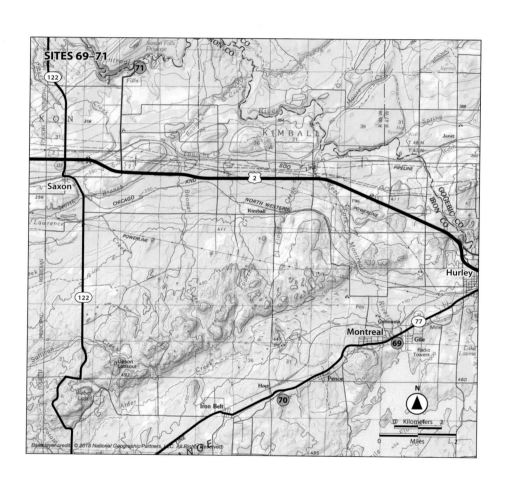

SITES 69–71

70. Plummer Mine Magnetite and Hematite

The Plummer Mine headframe is the last remaining headframe in the Wisconsin Gogebic Range.

County: Iron
Site type: Mine dump
Land status: Historical site, public access allowed
Material: Hematite and iron formation
Host rock: Early Proterozoic Menominee Group, Ironwood Iron Formation
Difficulty: Easy
Family-friendly: Yes
Tools needed: Hammer
Special concerns: Collecting status uncertain
Special attractions: None
GPS parking: N46° 24.467' / W90° 17.583'
GPS mine dump: N46° 25.500' / W90° 17.567'
Topographic quadrangle: Ironbelt, WI

The mine dump is loaded with magnetite and hematite.

Finding the site: From the intersection of US 51 and WI 77 in Hurley, take WI 77 west for 6.1 miles. Take the fork on the left (south) side of the highway. This fork is Plummer Road. Proceed southwest on Plummer Road for about 600 feet, and then turn left. Follow this dirt road to the parking area and you will see the Plummer Mine Headframe. The mine dumps are just northeast of the headframe. The mine dumps are about 200 feet north of the headframe and you can drive to them from the parking area.

Rockhounding

The Plummer Mine is an abandoned iron mine that worked iron ores from the Ironwood Iron Formation. The mine operated from 1905 to 1932, and produced about 172,000 tons of iron ore. The workings extended to nearly 2,400 feet below the surface. The mine is now a historic site. It has the only remaining mine headframe of all the mines in the Wisconsin Gogebic Range.

The mine headframe is nearly intact, and appears to be in good condition. The foundations and walls of buildings that used to support mining operations are not in good shape, and they are located south of the headframe in

Parts of the dump are stained red from all the hematite leaching from the rocks into the ground.

the woods. All that remains of these buildings is moss-covered concrete that has been overgrown with by trees and forest undergrowth.

The mine dump is easy to reach and is quite large. The dump is loaded with hematite and magnetite. Signs of the many previous rockhounds include pits dug into the dump and freshly broken rocks. The minerals on the dump are mainly hematite and magnetite. Given the red color of the dump, I had assumed that all the rocks were hematite. I was very surprised to find rocks rich in magnetite, and this was evident when I used a flashlight that had a magnet on the base of the flashlight. The magnet immediately stuck to the flashlight magnet. The magnetite pieces were generally very dense, flat slabs of red rock. The dump also has lots of specular hematite and this often forms bands in the rocks.

References: Cox, 2005; Wisconsin Historical Markers, 2015

71. Saxon Falls Zeolites in Precambrian Basalt

The zeolites are found in the outcrops in the Montreal River near the surge pipe for the hydroelectric plant.

County: Iron
Site type: Outcrop in Montreal River
Land status: Xcel Energy Saxon Falls Hydro Station Recreation Area
Material: Zeolites in basalt
Host rock: Middle Proterozoic Porcupine Volcanics
Difficulty: Easy
Family-friendly: Yes
Tools needed: Hammer and chisel
Special concerns: Rapidly changing water levels, waterfalls downstream
Special attractions: Saxon Falls
GPS parking: N46° 32.317' / W90° 22.483'

The zeolites often have a radiating pattern, especially in the larger amygdules.

GPS Zeolites: N46° 32.267' / W90° 22.583'
Topographic quadrangle: Little Girls Point, MI-WI
Finding the site: From the small town of Saxon, take WI 122 north. This is also known as Hoyt Road. Go 2.1 miles, and stay to the right when the road becomes Berg Street. Continue north for 0.4 mile, and turn right (east) on CR-B. Continue 1.5 miles, then turn left (north) onto Saxon Falls Road. Go 0.4 mile, and turn right (east) onto an unnamed road. Continue 0.6 mile to the end of road and park here. This is the dam site, and the zeolites are downstream of the dam.

Rockhounding

The Saxon Falls hydro power generating station was built in 1913, and was rebuilt in 1940. It has a power production capacity of 1.2 megawatts. The station is on the Wisconsin–Michigan border. It is a run–of–the–river surge tank operation, and a large pipe, which is nearly 1300 feet long, goes from the dam to the surge tank. The generating station is located on the Michigan side of the river downstream of the falls. The plant and dam are located in a deep canyon.

The main mineral of interest at this locality is the zeolite thompsonite, with occurs in the amygdules of the basalt of the Porcupine Volcanics. The zeolites are generally white to light green. When I visited the site in the summer of 2010, the best way to see the zeolites was to park near the dam and walk to the outcrops exposed in the Montreal River near the large surge pipe.

Many of the best exposures of zeolites are in the smooth outcrops of basalt and these are best left for viewing only, as hammering them out is practically impossible due to the hardness of the basalt and lack of rough sections to crack off. However, with a little effort you can find some pieces that can be separated from the main mass of the rock with a hammer and chisel. In addition to the white and light green zeolites I also found some red agate in some of the basalts.

This is obviously a site that is best viewed during low water in summer months. During high water or ice and snow, the Montreal River will be too dangerous. If you fall in the river you may go over the falls. The dam also has a warning sign that states that when the generators operate, an alarm will sound, and the water levels by the plant will increase and the waters will become very rough. The power plant is actually on the Michigan side of the Montreal River and downstream of the surge tank, so I am not sure if water levels immediately below the dam will also increase. I know for certain though that if I hear the alarm, I am immediately leaving the river for high ground.

Saxon Falls can be viewed by a moderately strenuous hike from the power plant area, but I did not get to see Saxon Falls on this trip. If you plan to see the falls, it appears that you will have to take the road toward the power plant, which is reached by continuing straight on Saxon Falls Road before you took the right on the unnamed road to get to the dam site. Satellite photos indicate parking is available on the Wisconsin side of the river. I have not been there and various online reports indicate some hiking and climbing are involved if you want to get a good view of Saxon Falls.

References: Cannon, 1996; Cordua, 1998; Sims, 1992; USGS, 2004

72. Mellen Rainbow Slaty Turbidites

The rocks in the outcrop are slaty and fissile, and are easily broken.

County: Iron
Site type: Roadcut
Land status: Uncertain, not posted
Material: Ferruginous argillite and iron formation
Host rock: Early Proterozoic Baraga Group Tyler Formation
Difficulty: Easy
Family-friendly: Yes
Tools needed: Hammer
Special concerns: Traffic
Special attractions: Copper Falls State Park
GPS parking: N46° 20.967' / W90° 30.167'
Topographic quadrangle: Mt. Whittlesey, WI

The roadcut is on the north side of the road and is easy to find.

Finding the site: From the intersection of WI 13 and WI 77 in Mellen, head east on WI 77 for 8.5 miles. The outcrops on the left (north) side of WI 77. Park on the north side of WI 77 next to the outcrops.

Rockhounding

This is an outcrop of the Early Proterozoic Tyler Formation of the Baraga Group. The Tyler Formation consists mainly of turbidites that were deposited in a foreland basin in front of accreting volcanic arcs to the south. Turbidites are clastic sediments formed as a result of turbidity currents that are loaded with mud and sand from underwater avalanches. They typically form in deep ocean environments.

At this location the rock is slaty and fissile, and it breaks into small flat pieces. It is not crystallized like many of the formations in the area, and pieces can be pulled out of the exposure by hand. The rock is not magnetic and does not have any distinct crystals, with the exception of a pyritic bed on the east side of the exposure.

The colors are seen on flat surfaces of freshly broken rock.

The unique feature of this outcrop is the colorful staining on broken surfaces. Many pieces have various shades of blue, green, and purple flat surfaces. This is likely due to dissolved iron and possibly minor copper that precipitated on these surfaces. The lower parts of the Tyler Formation are also reported to have sideritic shale.

The outcrops are reddish-brown at the surface. They do not have any further indications of significant copper mineralization, such as malachite staining, but green is one of the colors seen in the rocks. I have seen these colors before in other iron-mining districts. The color is likely due to dissolution of a variety of iron minerals that formed and were later oxidized in these rocks, and these original minerals may have included siderite, limonite, pyrite, magnetite, and hematite.

References: Cannon et al., 2007; USGS, 2004

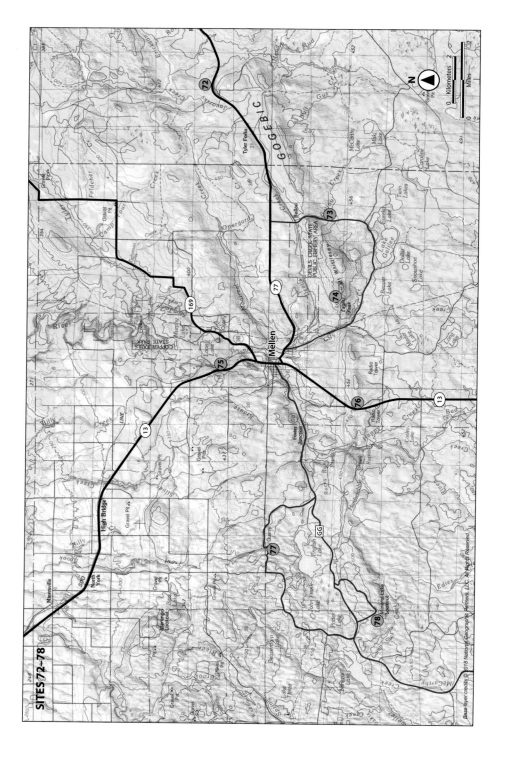

SITES 72–78

Base layer credits © 2018 National Geographic Partners, LLC. All Rights Reserved.

73. Ballou Creek Iron Formation

The road along Ballou Creek is narrow and parking is limited.

County: Ashland
Site type: Roadcut
Land status: Road right-of-way, not posted
Material: Iron formation
Host rock: Early Proterozoic Menominee Group, Ironwood Iron Formation
Difficulty: Easy
Family-friendly: Yes
Tools needed: Hammer
Special concerns: Road is narrow, limited parking
Special attractions: Caroline Lake State Natural Area
GPS parking: N46° 18.633' / W90° 34.650'
Topographic quadrangle: Mt Whittlesey, WI
Finding the site: From Mellen, take Lake Drive east for 0.4 mile, and turn left onto WI 77. Proceed 3.8 miles and then turn south (right) onto CR-MM.

The iron formation shows excellent banding.

Proceed 1.2 miles, and look for outcrops on the hills to the west (right). Ballou Creek is east of the road. Park on the east side of the road at about the 1.2 mile mark and walk to the outcrops on the west side of CR-MM.

Rockhounding

This site exposes outcrops of the Early Proterozoic Ironwood Iron Formation, which is part of the Menominee Group. Iron formation is a sedimentary rock that has at least 15 percent iron of sedimentary origin, and it often is thin-bedded or finely laminated. The rocks along Ballou Creek are reportedly iron-rich, and the rocks contain magnetite, hematite, and grunerite.

I had the opportunity to visit the outcrops along Ballou Creek in late June 2012. CR–MM is narrow but it is paved, and the outcrops are easy to see on the west side of the road. I was able to park on the east side of the road just south of the outcrops. The rocks dip steep to the west, and are finely bedded. Some of the rock appears to splinter, and this rock would likely not be great for construction aggregate as it will break into thin pieces as opposed to easily sized rocks.

Unfortunately I did not have a small magnet with me during my visit, so I could not verify if the rocks had magnetite. I observed that freshly broken surfaces of the rock showed finely bedded sediments, and the material had bands of dark gray to light gray. I did not see any red zones that would indicate the presence of hematite.

These rocks are within the Gogebic Range, which is a prominent range of iron formation that extends from northwestern Wisconsin into the Upper Peninsula of Michigan. High-grade iron ores were discovered in 1884–1886, and an iron-mining boom soon followed. From the late 1800s into the 1920s, iron mines from the Gogebic Range were a chief source of iron for American industry. Unfortunately, with the Great Depression many of the mines closed, resulting in economic devastation for the region. While some mines in the region continued to operate, they finally closed with the last shipment of ore to Granite City, Illinois in 1967.

Like all mining districts, the first ores taken out were the high-grade ores that required minimal processing. Despite decades of mining, there are still huge reserves of magnetite-rich taconite ores. In 2010, Gogebic Taconite, LLC began the exploration and permitting process for a new iron mine in the range. The mine would have been huge and was planned to be at least 1000 feet deep and nearly four miles long. It would have been the largest open pit mine in the world.

This project was huge and had lots of supporters and opponents. Despite the years of study and financial investment, Gogebic halted the project in 2015. They stated that the wetlands were too numerous for the mining to be economically feasible. While Gogebic is gone, other more experienced iron-mining companies are still looking at the area for smaller mines. Metallic mineral mining in Wisconsin is extremely difficult to get approved due to concerns about acid mine drainage, disposal of tailings, and other environmental issues.

References: Aldrich, 1929; Huber, 1959; Sims, 1992; Cordua, 1998; USGS, 2004

74. Berkshire Iron Mine Hematite and Ruins

The rocks at this mine site are well banded and have hematite-rich chert.

County: Ashland
Site type: Former Iron mine
Land status: Uncertain, not posted
Material: Iron formation
Host rock: Early Proterozoic Menominee Group, Ironwood Iron Formation
Difficulty: Easy
Family-friendly: Yes
Tools needed: Hammer
Special concerns: Access road may be rough
Special attractions: Copper Falls State Park
GPS parking: N46° 18.133' / W90° 37.383'
Topographic quadrangle: Mt. Whittlesey, WI

Abundant piles of mine rock can be found at the site.

Finding the site: From Mellen, take Lake Drive east. As you pass the intersection with WI 77, Lake Drive turns southeast. Go a total of 2.0 miles on Lake Drive, and you will see a small unmarked dirt road to the left. This road heads east toward Mount Whittlesey and Mellon Lookout tower. Proceed on this road for about 300 feet and take the fork to the left. Go approximately 1 mile, and you will see the ruins. Take the road to the north about 300 feet to the parking area, and mine rock piles of iron formation are around this area.

Rockhounding

This is an old mine site on the western end of the Gogebic Range. The ruins are on the west side of Mt. Whittlesey. The mine site was first work in 1886–1887 during the first iron boom in the range, and shafts were dug into the deposit. In 1917 the mine was sold and developed with an open pit, and ore was shipped from 1922 to 1924. The mine site was also likely to be part of a huge open pit mine that was in the permitting phase from 2010 to 2015, but the company developing the mine, Gogebic Taconite, cancelled the project in 2015 due to wetlands issues.

I am not sure how it got the name "Berkshire Mine," but that is the name shown on the topographic map. It also mentions "Ruins" on the map, so I knew this would be an intriguing site if I could get access. Fortunately, I was able to drive up to the mine site and ruins. There are some good rock piles with banded iron formation, and some of these rocks have red bands of hematite as well. This is an excellent location to get iron formation with abundant magnetite. The ruins are mainly the concrete walls of the former mine workings, and they are interesting to see in such a relatively remote area.

I visited this site in late June of 2012. At the time I had an SUV with all-wheel drive and decent clearance, and was able to make it up the road to the ruins. If the road is unpassable, it is only a 1-mile walk to the mine, and I think this site is worth hiking to if you cannot get there by vehicle. Since this is also a road to the Mellon Lookout Tower it may be maintained more than other roads in the area.

At the time I visited I did not have my smartphone and did not have the benefit of looking at satellite photo coverage. If you go to this site, it may be worth exploring further to the east, as the satellite photo indicates some large outcrops are present about 150 east of the ruins. A small lake, which may represent a former open pit, is present about 300 feet to the southwest of the ruins. Both of these areas warrant further exploration if you are in the area.

References: Cordua, 1998; USGS, 2004

75. Mellen Spotted Cow Rock

The black and white rocks in this roadcut give the appearance of a "spotted cow."

County: Ashland
Site type: Roadcut
Land status: Uncertain, not posted
Material: Black and white granitic rocks and pegmatites
Host rock: Precambrian granite of the Mellen Intrusive Complex
Difficulty: Easy
Family-friendly: Yes
Tools needed: Hammer
Special concerns: Traffic
Special attractions: Copper Falls State Park
GPS parking: N46° 20.700' / W90° 39.900'
Topographic quadrangle: Mellen, WI
Finding the site: From the intersection of Lake Drive and WI 13 in Mellen, head north on WI 13 for 1.5 miles. The outcrops of the "Spotted Cow Rock" will be on

Small pegmatites with feldspar crystals can also be found in this roadcut.

your left (west). Make a U-turn and park next to the outcrops so you do not have to cross the highway.

Rockhounding

This is an unusual outcrop just north of Mellen. The rocks are a granitic intrusion with abundant dark gneiss and dark granite xenoliths. The pattern resembles a spotted black and white cow. Most of the outcrops in this region are either iron formation or basaltic rocks, and this is one of the few granitic intrusions I have seen in this region.

The southern end of the outcrop also has some pegmatitic zones. Some of these have distinct feldspar crystals that have grown in the core of the pegmatite. Most of these are solid within the rock and cannot be broken out, so it best to leave them for future visitors.

Reference: USGS, 2004

76. Mellen Iron Formation

County: Ashland
Site type: Roadcut
Land status: Uncertain, not posted
Material: Iron formation
Host rock: Precambrian Ironwood Iron Formation
Difficulty: Easy
Family-friendly: Yes
Tools needed: Hammer
Special concerns: Traffic, small outcrop
Special attractions: None
GPS parking: N46° 17.617' / W90° 41.133'
GPS outcrops: N46° 17.650' / W90° 41.133'
Topographic quadrangle: Mellen, WI
Finding the site: From the intersection of Lake Drive and WI 13 in Mellen, head south on WI 13 for 2.5 miles. The outcrops of iron formation are on the right (east) side of WI 13. Park on the east side of WI 13 on shoulder of the road near the intersection of WI 13 and South Foley Road, and walk to the outcrop.

Rockhounding

This is a small but well-exposed outcrop of iron formation on the west end of the Gogebic Range. The outcrop is within the Precambrian Ironwood Iron Formation. The rock is fine grained, well foliated, and slaty. It breaks into flat pieces. It is difficult to get large pieces without them breaking into smaller fragments. The rocks show excellent banding. One of the minerals reported at this site is grunerite, which is an iron-rich amphibole. However, the rocks are so fine-grained that I was not able to distinguish if any of the minerals in the pieces I broke off the outcrop contained grunerite. To my surprise, the rocks at the outcrop were not magnetic when I checked them with a magnet.

The reported presence of grunerite in the rocks of the Ironwood Formation has caused some major problems in the permitting for new iron mines in the Gogebic Range. Grunerite is the iron-end member of the grunerite-cummingtonite series, and is considered an asbestiform mineral. Amosite is a rare asbestiform variety of grunerite that was mined as asbestos in South Africa. In fact, the origin of the mineral name amosite comes from AMOSA, which is an acronym for the mining company "Asbestos Mines of

The rocks are well foliated and break into flat pieces.

South Africa." Amosite is often known as "brown asbestos," and the fibers are typically much shorter and thicker than those of chrysotile asbestos.

As mentioned, I could not determine the presence of grunerite in hand samples from the outcrop, but I also did not have the benefit of observing the rock under a microscope. In the early days of iron mining in the region, companies would not have given grunerite a second thought, but those days are long gone.

References: Cordua, 1998; USGS, 2004

77. Kornstead Road Precambrian Gabbro Quarries

Many of the rocks in the quarry have large crystals of feldspar, hornblende, and augite.

County: Ashland
Site type: Former Quarries
Land status: Chequamegon-Nicolet National Forest
Material: Hornblende and augite in coarse anorthositic gabbro
Host rock: Middle Proterozoic Keweenawan Mellen intrusive complex
Difficulty: Easy
Family-friendly: Yes
Tools needed: Hammer
Special concerns: Deep water of quarry
Special attractions: English Lakes Hemlock State Natural Area
GPS parking-Main Quarry: N46° 19.517' / W90° 45.850'
GPS parking-Smaller Quarry: N46° 19.567' / W90° 45.767'
Topographic quadrangle: Mineral Lake, WI

Large gabbro boulders are on the north side of the quarry, which is now a lake.

Finding the site: From Mellen, take CR-GG for 3.9 miles. Turn right (north) onto Quarry Road. Proceed 1.7 miles, and turn left (west) on Kornstead Road. Continue 0.8 mile on Kornstead Road to the main quarry, which will be on your left and south of a sharp bend in the road. The parking area is very wide but the quarry is hard to see from the road, and you may drive by it if you are not watching. The smaller quarry is about 500 east of the main quarry, and you will have just passed it while going to the main quarry.

Rockhounding

This site is two quarries, but by far the best exposures of rocks and opportunities for collecting are in the main quarry, which is on the south side of Kornstead Road. This quarry is the same gabbro quarry that is often referenced as being on "Quarry Road," but the road name is actually Kornstead Road. It seems likely that the road may have been Quarry Road in the past as Quarry Road leads to Kornstead Road.

I visited the main quarry in May 2017. I was driving down Kornstead Road in a major thunderstorm, and it was hard to see the road. Just by chance

I drove by the entrance as the rain was letting up, and I pulled into a flat area for parking. The rain soon stopped and the sun came out, and I was able to get a good look at this quarry.

The quarry is now a lake, and the sides are lined with many large boulders of anorthositic gabbro. The gabbro is part of the Mineral Lake Intrusion, which is a Proterozoic-layered mafic complex. The gabbro is extremely coarse-grained, and large crystals of hornblende, augite, and plagioclase can be seen in the matrix. Coarse zones, when broken apart, often reveal wide elongated hornblendes and augites. These are generally dark green-gray to nearly black, and their cleavage and crystal planes reflect well in the sun.

The best way to find the large crystals is to look among the boulders and other rocks on the north side of the quarry next to the parking area. These rocks are extremely hard and it is difficult to break them apart.

In June 2012 I visited the smaller quarry. At the time there was some road construction and I did not drive further down the road to the larger quarry. I also did not have a smartphone back then so I could not see the larger quarry on a satellite view. The smaller quarry does not have as many large pieces of coarse-grained gabbro, and most of the pieces I saw here were fine-grained. However, it is still worth checking out when you are in the area.

I also saw that these quarries were reportedly "swimming holes." I do not recommend swimming here. The quarries look very deep and cold, and there is always the potential to encounter metal equipment foundations, sharp underwater ledges, or other hazards in the water. If you must swim, find a nearby lake with a public access beach. There are certainly plenty of lakes in Wisconsin.

References: Cordua, 1998; Fitz, 2011; Sims, 1992; USGS, 2004

78. Mineral Lake Tower Iron Formation

County: Ashland
Site type: Outcrops on ridge
Land status: Chequamegon National Forest
Material: Iron formation
Host rock: Early Proterozoic Menominee Group, Ironwood Iron Formation
Difficulty: Moderate
Family-friendly: Yes
Tools needed: Hammer
Special concerns: Uphill hike, remote country, bear potential
Special attractions: Mineral Lake and Potter Lakes
GPS parking: N46° 17.583' / W90° 48.233'
GPS tower site: N46° 17.067' / W90° 48.067'
Topographic quadrangle: Mineral Lake, WI
Finding the site: From Mellen, take CR-GG west for 7.7 miles. Watch for a small turnout on the left (south) side of the road. This is Mineral Lake Tower Road. The road is closed, so you will have to park here and hike to the top of the ridge. When you reach the top of the ridge, turn west, and follow the trail to the site of the former tower.

Rockhounding

This site name is somewhat misleading as it should say "former" tower, but some maps still show that the tower is present. This site is at the western end of the Gogebic Range, and much of the ridge is reportedly iron formation.

I hiked to this site in late May of 2017. I was able to find Mineral Lake Tower Road easily. Even if this road was not closed, I would not have attempted to drive up the road, as I only had a two-wheel-drive car. Even with four-wheel drive and good clearance I do not like to take the risk of getting stuck. My maps showed that it was only about 0.5 mile to the ridge, so I counted on an easy hike.

The road soon became steeper, and I realized that this was a fairly remote area. I also remembered that I had seen large black bears with cubs crossing the roads in northern Wisconsin, so I was now on guard against bears. I did not have a bell or other way to make noise, so I grabbed a large rock and beat

The iron formation has some red hematite and fine-grained specular hematite.

it with my hammer as I walked up the road. While this may have seemed silly, it worked, as I did not see any bears.

Unfortunately, as soon as I arrived at the top of the ridge, a massive thunderstorm arrived, and I was caught in a huge downpour. This was bad enough, but then the lightning started. My phone soon began beeping with alerts that lightning strikes were occurring nearby. There was no shelter except for the trees, and I was not crazy about standing next to trees in a thunderstorm. The lightning soon passed, but the rain continued and made it much more difficult to explore the ridge top.

The tower has been removed for some time, and I was able to see some stairs built into nearby rocks and at least one footer, but not many more signs of the tower. There are some outcrops on the ridge, but they are covered with moss and vegetation, so it is hard to see the rocks. It is not like a roadcut or mine site. Some of the rocks are polished, presumably by glaciers, and have a distinct metallic gray appearance with banding.

As soon as the rain began to let up, the mosquitoes came out in force. I had managed to leave my repellent in the car. This was becoming a challenging

Some of the rocks are polished and the fine-grained specular hematite resembles a metal surface.

trip. I was able to find some hematite and fine-grained specular hematite in the outcrop near the former tower, but I soon had to leave. I was soaked and the mosquitoes were making staying difficult.

This is not an easy site for collecting, but it is the opportunity to see the western end of the Gogebic Range and some massive outcrops, albeit moss-covered, of iron formation. I highly recommend visiting on a storm-free day and with lots of mosquito repellent.

References: Cordua, 1998; Fitz, 2011; Sims, 1992; USGS, 2004

79. Grandview Marble Quarry

Many of the rocks show excellent banding from the original dolostone.

County: Bayfield
Site type: Former quarry
Land status: Uncertain, not posted
Material: Tremolite and banded marble
Host rock: Metamorphosed Proterozoic Bad River Dolomite
Difficulty: Easy
Family-friendly: Yes
Tools needed: Hammer
Special concerns: Land Ownership uncertain, requires some hiking
Special attractions: Fairyland State Natural Area
GPS parking: N46° 17.367' / W90° 59.550'
GPS quarry: N46° 17.117' / W90° 59.200'
Topographic quadrangle: Marengo Lake, WI
Finding the site: From Grandview, take CR-D south for 3.2 miles, than turn left (east) onto Camp 8 Road, which is the same as WI 377. Continue east for 2.6 miles,

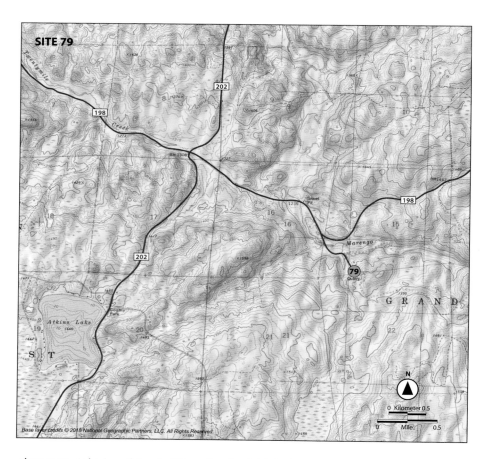

then turn right (south) onto Wisco Road, which is the same as WI 198. Continue 4.5 miles, and look for a small road on the right. Take a slight right onto this road, and proceed to a bridge across the Marengo River. Park here and hike approximately 1/3 mile to the quarry.

Rockhounding

This quarry is in a remote area. The quarry is within Proterozoic metamorphosed dolomite that is cut by Keweenawan (late Precambrian) basaltic dikes. It apparently got its name from Grandview, which is a small town to the northwest. The quarry was worked in the late 1950s by Wisconsin Marble Heights of Eau Claire, Wisconsin, and it produced a dolomitic marble. This was the only occurrence of marble in Wisconsin, and the company reportedly conducted studies and experiments to determine potential uses for this marble.

Radiating crystals of tremolite can be seen on many of the boulders.

I visited the quarry in late June 2012. The quarry had long been abandoned, and no mining equipment or signs of structures remained. There were many piles of white rocks and ridges of dolomite in the quarry, and the pine trees were well established. The rocks were a white to light gray banded dolomite. The basaltic dikes that cut the marble could also be seen in the quarry. Many of the white rocks were loaded with radiating splays of white to very light green tremolite.

This is one of those sites that has so many interesting rocks it is hard to know where to start, and most importantly, when to stop. The site is about 1/3 mile to your vehicle and you have to carry out any specimens that you may decide to collect. While the amount of material appears limitless, be sure to limit any collecting so future visitors can also see the unique tremolite and banded rocks at this quarry.

While some maps show this as National Forest Land, other maps show this as outside of the National Forest, which means that the site may be on private land. The woods on the side of the parking area are posted, but I did not see any other indications of private land near the quarry.

References: Cordua, 1998; Mudrey, 1979; Rand, 1959; USGS, 2004

80. Highway 27 Precambrian Basalt

This is one of the few outcrops on this section of the highway, and it is easy to find.

County: Bayfield
Site type: Roadcut
Land status: Uncertain, not posted
Material: Amygdaloidal basalt
Host rock: Precambrian Chengwatana Volcanic Group basalt
Difficulty: Easy
Family-friendly: Yes
Tools needed: Hammer
Special concerns: Remote location, traffic
Special attractions: None
GPS parking: N46° 15.083' / W91° 30.533'
GPS roadcuts: N46° 15.150' / W91° 30.550'
Topographic quadrangle: Ellison Lake, WI

The basalt has a spotted appearance from the green amygdules in the purplish-gray basalt.

Finding the site: From the intersection of WI 2 and WI 27, take WI 27 south for 23.1 miles. The outcrops will be on your right (west). Park off the road on the east side of the highway at a small unpaved drive to a cabin, but be sure not to block the driveway. You can then walk across the highway to the outcrops.

Rockhounding

This is a remote location, even though it is next to a well-built highway that receives a fair share of traffic. This outcrop has amygdaloidal basalt of the Precambrian Chengwatana Volcanic Group. On freshly broken surfaces the basalt is generally a brownish-red and has a spotted appearance due to amygdules, which are filled with light green minerals and white calcite. Secondary minerals reported at this site that likely fill the amygdules outcrop include chlorite, epidote, prehnite, natrolite, pectolite, and quartz.

While this location is remote, it is easy to reach if you have time to make the drive. I did not find any large vugs with crystals but many rockhounds and geologists have visited this outcrop as indicated by the many areas of broken

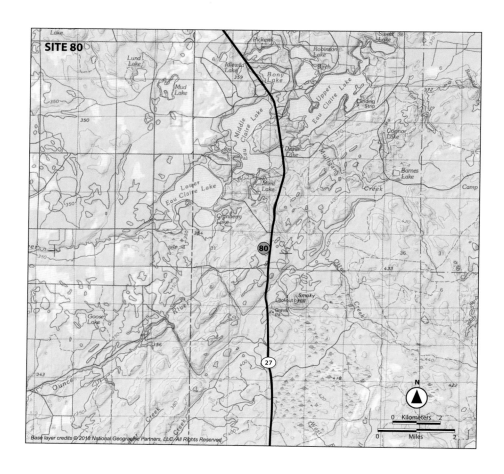

rocks. The easy pockets may have been identified and picked long ago, but with some persistence you may be able to find some zones with good crystals and attractive patterns in this outcrop.

References: Cordua, 1998; USGS, 2004

81. South Range Precambrian Basalt

The basalt is exposed on a small ridge on the west side of the road.

County: Douglas
Site type: Hillside outcrop along road
Land status: Uncertain, not posted
Material: Basalt
Host rock: Precambrian Chengwatana Volcanic Group basalt
Difficulty: Easy
Family-friendly: Yes
Tools needed: Hammer
Special concerns: Land status uncertain
Special attractions: Pattison State Park
GPS parking: N46° 34.467' / W91° 57.750'
Topographic quadrangle: South Range, WI

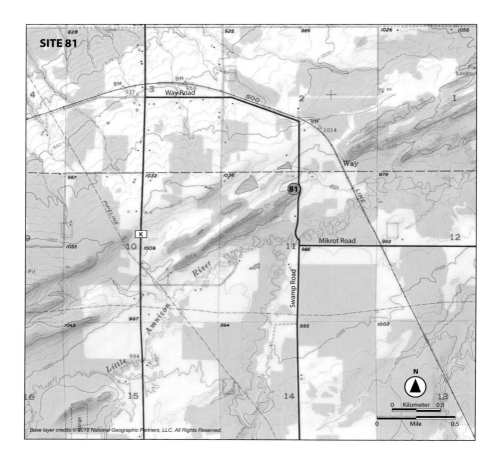

Base layer credits © 2018 National Geographic Partners, LLC. All Rights Reserved.

Finding the site: From US 53, take CR-C south 0.2 mile to CR-E, and turn right (west). Proceed 2.8 miles to Stone Road, and turn left (south). Continue 1.5 miles to Way Road, and turn left (east). Go 0.5 mile and turn right (south) onto Swamp Road. Go 0.4 mile and park on the shoulder of the road near a hillside. The basalt is exposed near the road on this hill.

Rockhounding

This is an outcrop of Precambrian basalt near the Little Amnicon River. We originally came to this area to look for amygdaloidal basalt in quarries located

Cavities filled with quartz crystals can be found in the basalt, but they are all but impossible to remove.

near Flanagan Lookout Tower. The tower is on a northeast trending ridge of basalt and is about 1.5 miles north of the site. Unfortunately, the quarries are active and posted against trespassing, and the road to Flanagan Lookout Tower is also closed to public access. However, during my pre-trip research I saw that the basalt ridge extended to the southwest. If the quarries were not accessible I thought this ridge could be worth checking out if access was possible.

The site is accessed by parking on the west shoulder of Swamp Road and walking up the hill. This area was not posted and the basalt is well exposed on the hillside. Freshly broken pieces can be found on the ground, and some of the surfaces of the basalt have weathered rinds that can be pried of with the pointed end of a rock hammer. The basalts have small amygdules, and many of these are weathered and hard to see. In some cases much larger vugs that are filled with quartz crystals occur in the basalt. These larger vugs are seen on flat sections of the basalt and are all but impossible to remove unless you have special tools, and even then it would be difficult.

References: Cordua, 1998; USGS, 2004

LAKE SUPERIOR LOWLAND

82. Amnicon River Beach

The waves on Lake Superior often bring in a lot of sand and this covers the agates.

County: Douglas
Site type: Lake Superior Beach
Land status: Amnicon River boat landing and beach
Material: Agates and beach pebbles
Host rock: Beach sediments derived from Proterozoic rocks
Difficulty: Easy and Difficult
Family-friendly: Yes
Tools needed: None
Special concerns: Agates are hard to find
Special attractions: Amnicon Falls State Park
GPS parking: N46° 41.467' / W91° 51.400'
Topographic quadrangle: Poplar NE, WI
Finding the site: From the intersection of US 53 and WI 13, take WI 13 east for 6.5 miles, then turn left (north) on Amnicon River Road, and go 3.3 miles to Lake Superior. Park here, and the beach is to your left (west).

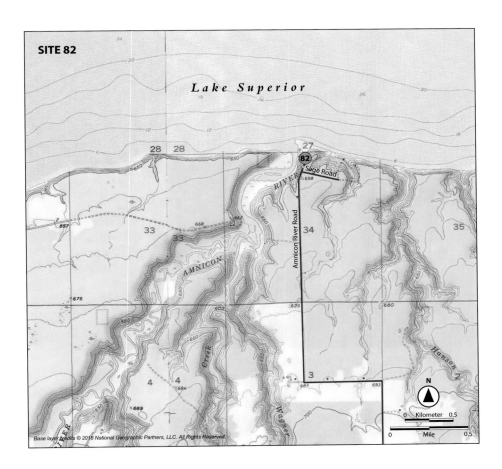

Lake Superior

Sage Road

Amnicon River Road

Base layer credits © 2018 National Geographic Partners, LLC. All Rights Reserved.

N

0   Kilometer   0.5

0   Mile   0.5

Rockhounding

This is a small beach where the Amnicon River empties into Lake Superior. The Amnicon River drains a wide area with basaltic rocks, and I thought that the basalts would have been a good potential source rock for Lake Superior agates. Lake Superior agates are a type of agate that is stained by iron oxides and has distinct banding. The quartz in the agate is cryptocrystalline and semitranslucent. The colors, especially the reds, are often intense and the agates are popular with collectors. Some of the best agates formed in the vesicles of the Precambrian basalt, so it made sense that this could be a good agate beach.

We visited this beach on a windy day in September 2017. The area had three cars at the parking area and it was difficult to find a space. However, one of the families visiting was leaving, and I was encouraged when a girl had a small plastic bucket of rocks she collected. When I asked her if she was

While the geology indicates this could be a good locality for agates, they remained elusive during this visit.

collecting agates, she said no, she was just collecting pretty rocks. She showed me what she found, but unfortunately none of them were agates.

We also met a guy who came back with a sack of rocks. He had picked up many rocks, but none of them were agates. He came to the site to kayak, but the water was far too rough. He said that the beach was good for finding agates, but the summer storms had buried all of the best rocks with sand. He said that it was best to come early in the spring after the winter ice had pushed all the rocks onto the beach. The ice apparently pushes material onto the beach, and this is the best time to find the agates.

We then went looking for agates ourselves. Unfortunately the beach was covered with recent sand from the waves, and we did not find any agates on this visit. However, given the favorable geology and access, this is a beach that should be checked again, especially in the spring.

References: Sims, 1992; USGS, 2004

83. Saxon Harbor Beach

The beach was very calm the day of my visit, but the cliffs are taking a beating from Lake Superior.

County: Iron
Site type: Lake Superior Beach
Land status: Saxon Harbor County Park
Material: Agates and beach pebbles
Host rock: Beach sediments derived from Proterozoic rocks
Difficulty: Easy and Difficult
Family-friendly: Yes
Tools needed: None
Special concerns: Agates are hard to find
Special attractions: Superior Falls just inside border with Michigan
GPS parking: N46° 33.717' / W90° 26.367'
GPS beach: N46° 33.750' / W90° 26.500'
Topographic quadrangle: Oronto Bay, WI-MI

This piece resembled an agate, but was actually a polished pebble of banded iron formation.

Finding the site: From the intersection of WI 122 and US 2 in just north of Saxon, take WI 122 north for 3.6 miles, then turn left (west) on CR-A. Proceed 1.4 miles, and park in the parking area to your right, which is the one nearest to the beach. From here you can walk to the beach, which is west of the parking area and along the Lake Superior shoreline.

Rockhounding

Saxon Harbor beach is a well-known agate collecting beach in Wisconsin. The beach is a public beach and parking is available. I visited this site in late May 2017 and was looking forward to finding lots of Lake Superior agates on the beach. Lake Superior agates are a type of agate that is stained by iron oxides and has distinct banding. The quartz in the agate is cryptocrystalline and semitranslucent. The colors, especially the reds, are often intense and the agates are popular with collectors.

At the time of my visit the access to the beach was blocked by driftwood. It took some effort to climb past the driftwood and this was a tripping hazard. There was also a family coming to the beach, and the father had a metal

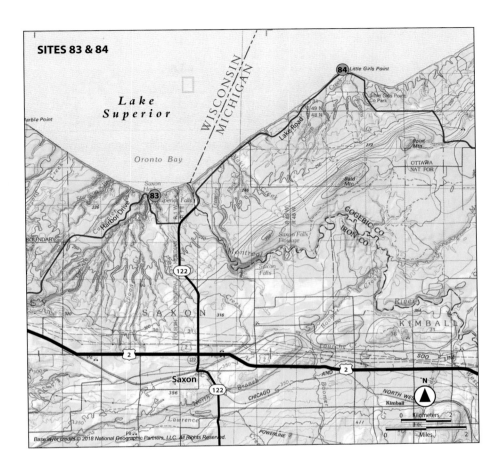

Lake
Superior

Oronto Bay

WISCONSIN
MICHIGAN

84 Little Girls Point

83

122

2

Saxon

122

2

N

Kilometers

Miles

Base layer credits © 2018 National Geographic Partners, LLC. All Rights Reserved.

detector. I was not sure what he would find here with a metal detector, but he confirmed that you could find agates on this beach. I soon walked west and had the entire beach to myself.

I watched the ground on the beach and at the wave line for indications of agates. Since I was new to this beach I thought it might take a while to identify the agates. The beach was full of pebbles and I thought for sure that I would soon find an agate. I found many colorful stones that I thought were agates, but I was mistaken. I found some small polished pebbles of banded iron formation, and these had layers that resembled the banding in Lake Superior Agates. A key difference was that the layers were nearly straight and were formed from sedimentary bedding instead of layers of quartz building over time during the formation of an agate. The banded iron formation pebbles

Looking west, the beach goes on for quite a distance.

were also opaque and not translucent. While these are not agates, they are still nice stones.

I continued to look hard for obvious agates, but I did not find any. Although you cannot be guaranteed to find agates at this location, you are guaranteed an accessible scenic beach with lots of attractive pebbles. In these types of collecting environments, it is often the new collector or small child that often finds the most sought after rocks, so it is possible that you may find a good agate right away if you come to this beach.

References: Sims, 1992; USGS, 2004

84. Little Girls Point Beach

At the time of my visit the area next to beach was under construction.

County: Gogebic (Michigan)
Site type: Lake Superior Beach
Land status: Little Girls Point County Park
Material: Agates and beach pebbles
Host rock: Beach sediments derived from Proterozoic rocks
Difficulty: Easy and Difficult
Family-friendly: Yes
Tools needed: None
Special concerns: Agates are hard to find
Special attractions: Superior Falls just inside border with Michigan
GPS parking: N46° 36.483' / W90° 19.767'
Topographic quadrangle: Little Girls Point, MI-WI
Finding the site: From the intersection of WI 122 and US 2 in just north of Saxon, take WI 122 north for 4.7 miles and cross over into Michigan. Continue another

5.7 miles, and the parking area for Little Girls County Park will be on your left. Park here and walk to the beach.

Rockhounding

Although this site is in Michigan, it is a well-known agate collecting beach and is so close to the border that it should be listed in this guide. The beach is a public beach and parking is available. I visited this site in late May 2017. There was a huge pile of rounded beach gravels next to the beach due to construction and I thought that this would have agates. Unfortunately the gravel consisted of a lot of rounded granitic and metamorphic rocks, and I did not find any agates. I scanned the shoreline and border of the waves for agates, but all I found were more rounded pebbles that I could tell were not agates.

The beach has lots of pebbles and but I did not see any obvious agates. I asked some of the visitors to the beach if they knew anything about the agates, but no one could tell me anything. I then saw a guy on all fours looking at beach pebbles. This guy was obviously looking for agates. I asked him if he had found anything. He said yes, but they were quite small. This was an understatement. They were extremely small red translucent agates, but they were less than ¼ inch in diameter. He said that it takes a lot of effort to find the agates, and they are often quite small.

I think the beach had been picked over quite a bit, even though it was late May and still early in the season. It would be best to come back after a major storm or after the ice has pushed more material onto the beaches. As you head east along the Michigan Upper Peninsula there are additional agate beaches, but they are outside of the scope of this book.

References: Sims, 1992; USGS, 2004

REFERENCES CITED

Agnew, Allen F., Heyl, Allen V., Jr., Behre, C. H., Jr., and Lyons, E. J., 1956. *Stratigraphy of Middle Ordovician Rocks in the Zinc-Lead District of Wisconsin, Illinois, and Iowa*. USGS Professional Paper 274-K.

Aldrich, Henry, 1929. *The Geology of the Gogebic Iron Range of Wisconsin*. Wisconsin Geological and Natural History Survey Bulletin, no. 71.

Bagrowski, B. P., 1940. *Occurrence of Millerite at Milwaukee. American Mineralogist* 25: 556–59.

Barrett, Joseph O., 1865. *History of "Old Abe" the Live War Eagle of the Eighth Regiment Wisconsin Volunteers*. Chicago: Dunlop, Sewell & Spalding.

Batten, W. G., and Attig, J. W., 2010. *Preliminary Geologic Map of Iowa County. Wisconsin*, Wisconsin Open File Report 2010–01, Plate 1.

Bayley, R. W., Dutton, C. E., Lamey, C. A., and Treves, S. B., 1966, "Geology of the Menominee Iron-Bearing District, Dickinson County, Michigan and Florence and Marinette Counties, Wisconsin, with a Section on the Carney Lake Gneiss." USGS Professional Paper 513.

Beard, Robert, 2002. "Wisconsin's Quartz Hill, Precambrian Gems Sparkle in the North Woods." *Rock & Gem Magazine*, May 2002.

Beard, Robert, 2010. "Wisconsin's Red Tourmaline, These Crystals Can Only Be Collected with Your Camera." *Rock & Gem Magazine*, May 2010.

Beard, Robert, 2015. *Rockhounding Delaware, Maryland, and the Washington D.C. Area*. Guilford, CT: FalconGuides.

Bostwick, Abigail M., and Hess, Anna N., 2015. "Digging Irma Hill and Krukoski Quarry." *Wisconsin Natural Resources Magazine*, February 2015.

Brown, Boyd A., (editor), 1983. "Three Billion Years of Geology: A Field Trip through the Archean, Proterozoic, Paleozoic and Pleistocene Geology of the Black River Falls Area of Wisconsin," in *Field Trip Guidebook* Vol. 9. Madison: Wisconsin Geological and Natural History Survey, 51 pp.

Brown, Boyd A., 1986. "Stop 2 Necedah Quartzite: The Wolf River Batholith and Baraboo Interval in Central Wisconsin," in *Field Trip Guidebook* Vol. 12. Madison: Wisconsin Geological and Natural History Survey, pp. 37–39.

Burgess, Phil, 2013. "Some Representative Fossils and Minerals of the Prairie du Chien Group in the Upper Mississippi Valley." *Rocks and Minerals* 88 (July–August 2013): 339–45.

Cannon, W. C., 1986. Bedrock Geologic Map of the Iron River 1° x 2° Quadrangle. Michigan and Wisconsin: US Geological Survey Miscellaneous Investigations Series Map I-1360-B, scale= 1:250,000.

Cannon, W. F., 1996. *Field Trip #2, Geology of the Montreal River Monocline: A Traverse through 25 km. of the Crust*: Institute on Lake Superior Geology, 42nd Annual Meeting, Proceedings, Pt. 3, Field Trip Guidebook: 49–63.

Cannon, W. F., LaBerge, G. L., Klasner, J. S., and Schulz, K. J., 2007. "The Gogebic Iron Range—A Sample of the Northern Margin of the Penokean Fold and Thrust Belt." US Geological Survey Professional Paper 1730, 44 p.

Chicago and North Western Railway Company, 1908. *A History of the Origin of the Place Names Connected with the Chicago & North Western and Chicago, St. Paul, Minneapolis & Omaha Railways*, Chicago and Northwestern Railway Company, p. 82.

Cordua, W. S., 1998. "Minerals of Wisconsin." *Rocks and Minerals* 73(6): 378–99.

Cox, B. 2005. *Mines of the Pewabic Country of Michigan and Wisconsin: Vol. 3 Wisconsin Iron.* Wakefield, MI: Agogeebic Press, pp. 115–17.

Cummings, M. L. 1984. "The Eau Claire River Complex: A Metamorphosed Precambrian Mafic Intrusion in Western Wisconsin." *Geological Society of America Bulletin* 95: 75–86.

Dalziel, I. W. D., and Dott, R. H. 1970. "Geology of the Baraboo District, Wisconsin." *Wisconsin Geological and Natural History Survey Information Circular* 14, 164 p., 7 plates.

Dapples, E. C., 1955. "General Lithofacies Relationship of St. Peter Sandstone and Simpson Group." *American Association of Petroleum Geologists Bulletin* 39: 444–67.

Dott, Robert H., and Attig, John W., 2004. *Roadside Geology of Wisconsin.* Missoula, MT: Mountain Press.

Dutch, Steven, 2013. *Wequiock Falls,* at https://www.uwgb.edu/dutchs/GeologyWisconsin/geostops/wequiock.htm, accessed 2017.

Dutton, Carl E., 1971. "Geology of the Florence Area, Wisconsin and Michigan." US Geological Survey Professional Paper 633.

Eckert, Allan W., 2000. *Earth Treasures Volume 1, The Northeastern Quadrant.* Lincoln, NE: iUniverse.com.

EMSL Analytical Inc., 2017. "Amosite Asbestos," available at https://www.emsl.com/Page.aspx?id=373, accessed 2017.

Evans, T. J., 2004. *Preliminary Bedrock Geologic Map of Racine County, Wisconsin.* Wisconsin Geologic and Natural History Survey Open-File Report 2004-12A.

Falster, A., 1986. "Minerals of the Stettin Pluton, Marathon County, Wisconsin." *Rocks and Minerals* 61(2): 74–78.

Fitz, Thomas, 2011. "57th Annual Meeting, Institute of Lake Superior Geology," in *Field Trip Guidebook, Proceedings* Volume 57, Part 2—Field Trip Guidebook, Field Trip 9, Granitic, Gabbroic, and Ultramafic Rocks of the Keweenawan Mellen Intrusive Complex, published by the Institute on Lake Superior Geology.

Ham, Nelson R., and Attig, John W., 1997. "Pleistocene Geology of Lincoln County." *Wisconsin Bulletin* 93, 31 pp.

Harms, Carl, 1991. "History of Lime Kiln Park," available at www.village.grafton.wi.us/DocumentCenter/Home/View/604, accessed 2017.

Hess, Julie A. M., Hess, Robert J., Hess, Anna N., and Bostwick, Abigail M., 2017. "Shadows of a Cambrian Shoreline: Saddle Mound through the Ages." *Wisconsin Natural Resources,* February 2017.

Heyl, Allen V., Jr., Lyons, Erwin J., and Agnew, Allen F., 1951. "Exploratory Drilling the Prairie du Chien Group of the Wisconsin Zinc-Lead District by the U.S. Geological Survey in 1949–1950." *USGS Circular 131,* 1951.

Heyl, A., and West, W. S., 1982. "Outlying Mineral Occurrences Related to the Upper Mississippi Valley Mineral District, Wisconsin, Iowa, Illinois, and Minnesota." *Economic Geology* 77: 1803–17.

Kimball, K., and Spear, F., 1984. "Metamorphic Petrology of the Jackson County Iron Formation, Wisconsin." *Canadian Mineralogist* 22: 605–19.

Hess, J., and Hess, A., 2017. "Waters Run Deep at Lake Wazee." *Wisconsin Natural Resources Magazine* 41(3): 14–16.

Huber, N. King, 1959. "Some Aspects of the Origin of the Ironwood Iron Formation of Michigan and Wisconsin." *Economic Geology* 54: 82–118.

International Movie Database (IMDb), 2017. Samuel L. Jackson (Neville Flynn) quote from *Snakes on a Plane,* available at www.imdb.com/title/tt0417148/quotes, accessed 2017.

Johnson, David, 2017. "Wisconsin Mines," available at www.miningartifacts.org/Wisconsin-Mines.html, accessed 2017.

Johnson, Robert W., 1958. *Geology of the Little Commonwealth Area, Florence County, Wisconsin.* US Geological Survey Open File Report, 58–53.

LaBerge, G. L., and Myers, P. E., 1972. *1971 Progress Report on Mapping of Precambrian Geology of Marathon County, Wisconsin.* Wisconsin Geological and Natural History Survey Open File Report, unpaginated.

LaBerge, G. L., and Myers, P. E., 2008. "Precambrian Geology of Marathon County, Wisconsin: Digital Information." *Information Circular 45-DI.*

Lackey, Brenda, Gross, Michael, Zimmerman, Ron, and Buchholz, Jim, 2009. *Rib Mountain State Park, Conceptual Master Plan for an Educational and Interpretative Center,* submitted to Friends of Rib Mountain State Park, prepared by Schmeeckle Reserve Interpreters, https://www.uwsp.edu/cnr-ap/schmeeckle/Documents/Consulting/Rib_Mountain_plan.pdf, accessed 2017.

Laybourn, D. P., 1979. *Geology and Metamorphism of the Ironwood Iron Formation, Gogebic Range, Wisconsin.* University of Minnesota–Duluth, unpublished M.S. thesis, 223 p.

LePain, David L., 2006. *Preliminary Geologic Map of the Buried Bedrock Surface of St. Croix County, Wisconsin.* Wisconsin Geological and Natural History Survey Open-File Report 2006-04.

McDonald, Cory, Baker-Muhich, Brandy, Fitz, Tom, Garrison, Paul, Petchenik, Jordan, Rasmussen, Paul, Thiboldeaux, Robert, Walker, William, and Watras, Carl, 2013. *Taconite Iron Mining in Wisconsin: A Review.* Madison: Wisconsin Department of Natural Resources, Bureau of Science Services, December 2013.

Mudrey, M. G., Jr., 1979. "Middle Precambrian Geology of Northern Wisconsin," in *Field Trip Guidebook* Vol. 4. Madison: Wisconsin Geological and Natural History Survey, 44 p.

Mudrey, M. G., Jr., Brown, B. A., and Greenberg, J. K., 1982. "Bedrock Geologic Map of Wisconsin." University of Wisconsin–Extension, Geological and Natural History Survey, scale= 1:1,000,000.

Myers, P., Maye, E. R., Cummings, M. L., and Maercklein, D. R., 1974. "Precambrian Rocks of the Chippewa Region, Wisconsin," in *38th Annual Tri-State Geological Field Conference Guidebook,* edited by P. E. Myers. Eau Claire: University of Wisconsin, pp. 35–39.

Myers, Paul E., Sood, Mohan K., Berlin, Louis A., and Falster, A. U., 1984. Annual Institute on Lake Superior Geology Field Trip #3. The Wausau Syenite Complex of Central Wisconsin, April 28, 1984, Wausau, Wisconsin.

Nehm, Ross H., and Bemis, Bryan E., 2002. "Common Paleozoic Fossils of Wisconsin." Wisconsin Geological and National History Survey, Educational Series 45.

Ostrom, M.E., 1987. "St. Lawrence and Jordan Formations (Upper Cambrian) South of Arcadia, WI," in *DNAG Centennial Field Guide, North-Central Section* Vol. 3, edited by D. L. Biggs. Boulder, CO: Geological Society of America, pp. 191–94.

Owen, David D., 1852. *Report of a Geological Survey of Wisconsin, Iowa, and Minnesota; and Incidentally of a Portion of Nebraska Territory.* Made under instructions from the United States Treasury Department. Philadelphia, PA: Lippincott, Grambo.

Rand, Lenox, H., 1959. *The Mineral Industry of Wisconsin.* U.S. Bureau of Mines, Minerals Yearbook Area Reports.

Runkel, A. C., 1994. "Deposition of the Uppermost Cambrian (Croixan) Jordan Sandstone, and the Nature of the Cambrian-Ordovician Boundary in the Upper Mississippi Valley." *Geological Society of America Bulletin* 106: 492–506.

Runkel, A. C., 2000. *Sedimentology of the Upper Cambrian Jordan Sandstone: A Classic Cratonic Sheet Sandstone Deposited during Regression in a "Typical" Marine Setting.* Guidebook for 30th Annual Field Conference, Great Lakes Section for the Society for Sedimentary Geology, p. 43–46.

Saggio, Mary, 2017. "History of Hazel Green, Wisconsin, (1881)," available at http://genealogytrails.com/wis/grant/history_hazelgreen.htm, accessed 2017.

Sapulski, Wayne S., 2001. *Lighthouses of Lake Michigan: Past and Present.* Manchester, MI: Wilderness Adventure Books.

Schmidt, R. G., 1980. "The Marquette Range Supergroup in the Gogebic Iron District, Michigan and Wisconsin." *US Geological Survey Bulletin* 1460: 96 p.

Schulz, K., and LaBerge, G., 2003. *Field Trip 1—Wausau-Pembine Terrane Institute of Lake Superior Geology*, Annual Proceedings, vol. 49, pt. 2, p. 33–46.

Sims, P. K., 1990. "Geologic Map of Precambrian Rocks of Eau Claire and Green Bay 1° x 2° Quadrangles, Central Wisconsin," US Geological Survey Miscellaneous Investigations Series Map I-1925, scale = 1:250,000.

Sims, P. K., Klasner, J. S., Day, W. C, and Peterman, Z., 1991. *Field Trip #1: The Mountain Shear Zone, Oconto County., Wisconsin: A Post-Penokean Discrete Ductile Deformation Zone.* 39th Annual Institute of Lake Superior Geology Proceedings, pt. 2, p. 1–32.

Sims, P. K., Schulz, K. J., and Peterman, Z. E., 2012. "Geology and Geochemistry of Early Proterozoic Rocks in the Dunbar Area, Northeastern Wisconsin." US Geological Survey Professional Paper 1517.

Sirbescu, M. L. C., Hartwick, E. E., and J. J. Student, 2008. "Rapid Crystallization of the Animikie Red Ace Pegmatite, Florence County, Northeastern Wisconsin: Inclusion Microthermometry and Conductive-Cooling Modeling." *Contributions to Mineralogy and Petrology* 156: 289–305.

Sivon, P. A., 1979. "The Stratigraphy and Paleontology of the Maquoketa Formation (Upper Ordovician) at Wequiock Creek, Eastern Wisconsin." Geological Society of America, abstracts with programs, vol. II, no. 5, p. 257.

Summers, W. K., 1965. "Geology and Ground-Water Resources of Waushara County, Wisconsin." US Geological Survey Water-Supply Paper 1809B, 32 p.

Swanson, Carl, 2015. "Estabrook Park Is a Reminder of Milwaukee's Mining Days," available at https://milwaukeenotebook.com/2015/01/12/milwaukees-mining-days/, accessed 2017.

Syverson, Kent M., Runkel, Anthony C., and Brown, Bruce, 2012. "Stop 4, Jordan Formation, Highway 93 Roadcut South of Arcadia, 2012," in *Field Guidebook on the Silica Sand Resources of Western Wisconsin*, Conference on the Silica Sand Resources of Minnesota and Wisconsin, October 1–3, 2012, PRC Guidebook 12-01.

Thwaites, F. T., and Lentz, R. C., 1922. *Bedrock Geology of Door County, Wisconsin*, Wisconsin Geological Survey Open-File Report WOFR1922-02-map01.

Twenhofel, W. H., 1936. "The Greensands of Wisconsin." *Economic Geology* 31: 472–487.

USGS Open-File Report, 2004. *2004-1355 Integrated Geologic Map Databases for the United States; the Upper Midwest States: Minnesota, Wisconsin, Michigan, Illinois, and Indiana*, http://pubs.usgs.gov/of/2004/1355/.

Whitlow, Jesse W., and West, Walter S., 1966. "Geology of the Potosi Quadrangle, Grant County, Wisconsin, and Dubuque County, Iowa," US Geological Survey Bulletin 1123-I.

Whitlow, Jesse W., and West, Walter S., 1966. "Geologic Map of the Dickeyville Quadrangle, Grant County, Wisconsin, GQ 488," US Geological Survey, 1966.

Wicklund, Peter, 2001. "He Sold Malted Milk; Horlick's Business Was People," available at http://journaltimes.com/news/local/he-sold-malted-milk-horlick-s-business-was-people/article_678750d1-57de-50a1-88a7-6d736c21fa29.html, accessed 2017.

Wisconsin Historical Markers, 2012. "Leathem and Smith Quarry," available at www.wisconsinhistoricalmarkers.com/2012/09/marker-417-leathem-and-smith-quarry.html, accessed 2017.

Wisconsin Historical Markers, 2015. "Penokee Iron Range Trail: Plummer Mine Geologic Layer Cake," available at www.wisconsinhistoricalmarkers.com/2015/06/penokee-iron-range-trail-plummer-mine.html, accessed 2017.

SITE INDEX

ABOUT THE AUTHOR

Robert Beard is a geologist and has collected rocks for over thirty years. He received his BA in geology, with a minor in mathematics, from California State University, Chico, in 1983 and his MS in geology from the University of New Mexico in 1987. He is a licensed professional geologist in Pennsylvania and works as an environmental consultant. He has collected rocks throughout the United States, in the Caribbean, and in southern Europe. He is a contributor to *Rock & Gem* magazine and has written for *Rock & Gem* since 1993. His most recent books for FalconGuides include *Rockhounding Pennsylvania and New Jersey*, published in 2013; *Rockhounding New York*, published in 2014; *Rockhounding Delaware, Maryland, and the Washington, DC Metro Area*, published in 2015; and *Rockhounding Virginia*, published in 2017. He and his wife, Rosalina, live in Harrisburg, Pennsylvania, with the Chihuahuas Nema and Little One, and Lennon the cat.

Credit: Rosalina Beard